Vintage Cookbooks

and Advertising Leaflets

Sandra J. Norman
and Karrie K. Andes

Schiffer Publishing Ltd

4880 Lower Valley Road, Atglen, PA 19310 USA

Disclaimer

All of the information in this book, including values, has been compiled from reliable sources and every effort has been made to eliminate errors and questionable data. Nevertheless, the possibility of error in a work of such immense scope always exists. Neither the publisher nor the authors will be held responsible for losses which may occur in the purchase, sale, or other transaction of items because of the information contained herein. Readers who feel they have discovered errors are invited to write and inform the publisher or authors, so that changes can be made in subsequent editions.

Designed by Laurie A. Smucker
Type set in *Seagull Hv BT/Aldine721 BT*

ISBN: 0-7643-0621-9
Printed in China

Published by Schiffer Publishing Ltd.
4880 Lower Valley Road
Atglen, PA 19310
Phone: (610) 593-1777; Fax: (610) 593-2002
E-mail: Schifferbk@aol.com
Please write for a free catalog.
This book may be purchased from the publisher.
Please include $3.95 for shipping.
Please try your bookstore first.

In Europe, Schiffer books are distributed by
Bushwood Books
6 Marksbury Avenue
Kew Gardens
Surrey TW9 4JF England
Phone: 44 (0)181 392-8585; Fax: 44 (0)181 392-9876
E-mail: Bushwd@aol.com

We are interested in hearing from authors
with book ideas on related subjects.

Contents

Dedication

This book is dedicated to the memory of my mother, Helen E. Herrin. Her encouragement and inspiration continues to guide me through every accomplishment.

Sandra Norman

This book is dedicated to my husband Robert for the countless number of hours spent on photography and traveling, for his amazing ability to recall books in the collection, and for loving me unconditionally.

Karrie Andes

Acknowledgments

I wish to thank my husband Carl for his patience, loyal support, and always lending a helping hand wherever it was needed. Special thanks to my friends Jill Massey and Sue Watson for always listening and enjoying collecting with me, and to Glenda Ryall who provided editing assistance and long distance moral support. I also wish to thank all the concerned and resourceful employees of the Research Department of the North Branch, Mid-Continent Public Library in Independence, Missouri for all their help and assistance.

Sandra Norman

Many thanks go to Nick and Nancy DeShetler of Grand Rapids, Ohio for allowing us to photograph their collection and helping to provide accurate values. You both are great! Thanks to James Welsh, Jr., Independence, Missouri, for sharing some books from his wonderful collection.

A big thank you to Judy Sanell who provided me with enthusiastic support over the past year and helped us make things "sound good." Thanks to John and Linda Andes, my in-laws, for their continued encouragement. Steve Dinwiddie, you have superb technical talent! Sharon Roxburg, Edna Sheets, and Mary Ann Fulner, thanks so much for always being positive.

Karrie Andes

Chapter 1 Introduction

The field of collecting paper advertising memorabilia is enormous and there are literally hundreds of areas for collectors to choose from. In America, advertising has always been a means of promoting and selling products to the public. Ideas were translated through various forms of media such as newspapers, magazines, store displays, trade cards, and cookbooks. With the advances in color lithography and photography in the late 1800s and the competitive artistic market of the early 1900s, some of the most attractive and charming paper collectibles were created.

Through the introduction of cookbooks and recipe pamphlets, companies achieved brand name exposure while providing the consumer with new and exciting ways to use their products. New discoveries and inventions required instructions to educate the cook, teaching them how to prepare various foods and use new appliances and products especially made for the kitchen.

Cookbooks were distributed in various ways over the years. Early entrepreneurs used the horse and buggy to provide transportation, bringing their products and cookbooks to the rural farmlands, where they were eagerly greeted by customers. Local grocers were also given an ample supply, used as an incentive for consumers to purchase their goods, and some small cookbooks were included in the packaging. Later, as postal mail advanced, cookbooks were offered to the consumer through the redemption of coupons which were included with the purchase of a product, or by advertisements in magazines and newspapers.

International exposure for a company was easily achieved by exhibiting at expositions or world's fairs. Companies constructed elaborate and expensive displays to attract attendees, giving free samples and recipe books. Some companies even made their products come to life by traveling across the country on trains, stopping in various cities and towns. Consumers greeted these visits with parades and marching bands, and were anxious to meet costumed characters such as Aunt Jemima or the Quaker Oats pilgrim.

Another form of advertising distribution was achieved through the production of children's books. These playful publications provided entertainment and amusement to children, while familiarizing the housewife with new products and recipes.

Famous culinary authors such as Fannie Merritt Farmer, Marion Harland, and Sarah Tyson Rorer were hired by food manufacturers to endorse and publish recipes and products in their cookbooks. When radio programs became popular in the 1920s, companies commissioned well-known celebrities such as Kate Smith or Jack Benny to entertain, sell, and give away cookbooks on the air.

Collecting cookbooks can not only be a fun and rewarding hobby, it also provides us with a window to America's past. Cookbooks give us an elaborate view of history through the years and the constantly changing environment of the kitchen. Each explains how we prepared our meals, cooked and served our food, and taught social manners of style, dress, and behavior. Cookbooks also give us insight into the economic conditions of our country, especially under the stress of war and depression. Whether you are an expert cook, a history buff, or just love collecting antiques, there are hundreds of cookbooks waiting to be discovered!

How This Book is Organized

The primary goal of cookbooks and advertising pamphlets was to familiarize the public with the brand names of the products. You can easily locate a cookbook in this guide by identifying the brand name. The first half of the book includes food brands, listed in alphabetical order in column format. You will also find chapters dedicated to die-cut cookbooks, media, children's books, black memorabilia, and wartime cookbooks. In addition, medicines, tonics, life insurance, and publications are categorized for easy reference. The final chapter includes cookware, products, and appliances, organized by brand names as well. If you have difficulty locating an item, refer to the handy index in the back of this book to find brands, company names, authors, or artists.

Where to Get Started

We have a hunch that a number of wonderful antique cookbooks in this country are snuggled in old kitchen cupboards or drawers, or lying forgotten in attics. Unfortunately, you can't just knock on doors and ask to snoop through people's homes, so we have some more conventional ideas for fulfilling your collection. Read on...

Sales

One of the easiest ways to start a collection is to find yard, garage, or church sales. You never know exactly what you're going to find, but the chances are good for finding cookbooks. If we had a quarter for every dingy, dusty, mildewed box we've dug though, we'd be rich by now! Estate sales also bring pleasant surprises as relatives go through the kitchen and sell items priced to go. If you plan a whole day hopping from one sale to another, you are bound to come home with a pile of cookbooks.

Auctions

Residential auctions can be fun, although you'll need to devote most of the day. Depending on what you find, it could be several hours before the auctioneer steers towards that one special box under the table (of course, diehard collectors like us would wait for hours—anything to get a rare book!)

In addition, we've had lots of success purchasing cookbooks right from our own computer. Auction web sites on the Internet offer the convenience of shopping for collectibles all around the world, without ever having to leave your home.

Retail Shops and Shows

Of course, you can't leave out antique shops, antique malls, and countless numbers of antique shows and flea markets. On one occasion, we traveled nine hundred miles to attend an outdoor flea market that was located in Iowa. It was rainy and cold, and the market was located on an old horse race track. We tromped through six inches of Iowa mud and didn't find much to brag about. The end result was a carload of tired and cold collectors, but if we didn't venture out, we'd have to live with the thought that we might have missed something special.

Our best luck has been with antique advertising shows, paper collectible shows, or postcard shows. The Fort Washington, Pennsylvania show and the Indianapolis, Indiana shows are wonderful! These paper vendors travel from all over the country to attend these popular events. You can count on finding some rare books, but do be prepared to pay a fair price.

Chapter 2 Easy Identification

Identification of cookbooks can be an easy task the majority of the time. As you continue to collect you will become more familiar with indicators such as language, clothing, hairstyles, and appliances that were used in different decades. However, there are cookbooks which, unfortunately, simply defy a date and may require more time to identify. This is when you need to become a bit of a detective, and we have included some tips for quick identification as well as other information to make this task a little easier.

Searching for Dates

Most hard cover and soft cover books come with a copyright date. They are usually located on the inside title page at the bottom or on the back side of the title page. We have also found copyright dates in very small print on the bottom of either the front or back covers of many soft cover books.

There may be a date listed on the last page of a booklet or leaflet, such as "10-02." This simply indicates the month or day plus the last two digits of the year of publication. In this case, 10-02 means October, 1902.

If copyrights cannot be found, we suggest you look for any other dates in the book. Perhaps the advertisers may refer to a certain date in an article or a letter from one of their customers, which was common practice. Companies also referred to various Pure Food Laws that were passed in 1906. Through these laws, chemicals and the adulteration of food was brought to the attention of the government to protect the public's health against unsafe or unsanitary conditions. Any printed dates you can find will provide time frames for that particular book.

Awards and Medals: World's Fairs

Many food manufacturers were proud to display the various awards and medals they had received in expositions and world fairs, both nationally and internationally. The purpose of such events was to promote trade and introduce new products to the public. Each manufacturer competed for the many ribbons, plaques, and medals that were available. Winning these awards meant precious endorsements that lasted for decades, like Gold Medal Flour. If the latest medal was not illustrated inside, it was often mentioned on the next publication. We have included the following table of all major fairs and events for reference.

World's Fair and Expositions

Year	Name	City Located	Year	Name	City Located
1851	The Great Exhibition of the Works of Industry of All Nations	London, England	1907	Jamestown Ter-Centennial Exposition	Norfolk/Hampton Roads, Virginia
1853	Exhibition of the Industry of all Nations	New York, New York	1909	Hudston-Fulton Celebration	New York, New York
1855	Universal Exposition	Paris, France	1909	Alaska-Yukon Pacific Exposition	Seattle, Washington
1862	International Exposition	London, England	1910	Brussels International	Brussels, Belgium
1867	Paris Universal Exhibition	Paris, France	1915	Panama-Pacific International Exposition	San Francisco, California
1873	Universal Exhibition	Vienna, Austria	1915	Panama-California Exposition	San Diego, California
1876	U. S. International Centennial Exhibition	Philadelphia, Pennsylvania	1924-25	British Empire Exhibition	Wembley, England
1878	Paris Universal Exhibition	Paris, France	1925	International Exposition of Decorative Arts & Modern Industries	Paris, France
1879	Sydney International Exhibition	Sydney, Australia	1926	Sesqui-Centennial International Exposition	Philadelphia, Pennsylvania
1883	Foreign Exhibition	Boston, Massachusetts	1929	International Exposition	Barcelona and Seville, Spain
1883	Southern Exhibition	Louisville, Kentucky	1930	Stockholm International	Stockholm, Sweden
1884-85	World's Industrial & Cotton Centennial Exposition	New Orleans, Louisiana	1931	French Colonial Exposition	Paris, France
1889	International Universal Exposition	Paris, France	1933-34	Century of Progress International Exposition	Chicago, Illinois
1893	World's Columbian Exposition	Chicago, Illinois	1935	International Exposition	Brussels, Belgium
1894	California Mid-Winter International Exposition	San Francisco, California	1935	California-Pacific International Exposition	San Diego, California
1895	Cotton States & International Exposition	Atlanta, Georgia	1936-37	Great Lakes Exposition	Cleveland, Ohio
1897	International Exposition	Brussels, Belgium	1936-37	Texas Centennial Central Exposition	Dallas, Texas
1898	Trans-Mississippi Exposition	Omaha, Nebraska	1937	Arts & Techniques Exposition	Paris, France
1900	International Universal Exposition	Paris, France	1938	British Empire Exposition	Glasgow, Scotland
1901	Pan-American Exposition	Buffalo, New York	1939-40	Golden Gate International Exposition	San Francisco, California
1904	Louisiana Purchase Exposition	St. Louis, Missouri	1939-40	New York World's Fair	New York, New York
1905	Louis & Clark Centennial Exposition	Portland, Oregon			

World Wars

Food companies and their cookbooks reflected the history of our country during these wartime eras. They suggested solutions to cope with the economic and social conditions of the time. During World War I (1914-1918) and World War II (1939-1945) many food items were in short supply or rationed, such as meat, wheat, sugar, and butter to name a few. The recipes in cookbooks from these years were designed to substitute, use less, or totally eliminate scarce ingredients while still promoting the company's products.

Famous Culinary Authors and Artist Signatures

Many famous authors, especially the very early pioneers of culinary literature, have had their accomplishments fully documented. You can locate dates for certain events mentioned in cookbooks, such as establishing or becoming principal of a prominent cooking school, or becoming a spokesperson and endorsing food products for companies. Famous artists were also commissioned to design the covers of many cookbooks. You can find this information by researching it at your local library or by using the bibliographies we have listed in the back of this book.

Identifying Fashions and Appliances

Learn to familiarize yourself with different dress and hair styles over the years. There is quite a difference in the starched, prim and formal look of ladies from the 1890s—dressed in high collars, long dresses, mutton-like sleeves, and hair up in buns—from those of later years. After the 1930s, fashion had a more relaxed look, which included short skirts, bobbed hairstyles, and many other fashion crazes.

Kitchen furniture and cabinet styles, along with their decorative colors, changed too. Appliances such as wood and oil stoves from the turn of the century evolved into the electric range, which became popular in the 1930s and 1940s. Electric refrigerators promoted in the 1940s were a boom to the food industry—a far cry from the ice boxes of yesterday. You can find excellent books on American chronology, which offer illustrated views through the years, at your local library or book store.

Beware of Reprints

Every year, more and more of the earliest hard cover cookbooks by famous authors are reprinted. Reprints are nice to own if you intend to keep a fragile original from being damaged. Also, the earlier versions may be more expensive and these reprints give an opportunity to browse through old recipes. Not all reprints indicate on the inside cover that they have been duplicated. One of the easiest ways to tell a modern reprint from an original is the scent from inside the book. Most reprints will have a chemical smell, quite different from the musty scent which comes from age. In addition, older hard cover books will usually have some wear on the corners and spine, and perhaps some foxing on the edges and inside pages. Foxing causes a reddish discoloration on the paper. Finally, the staples on older soft cover books will not appear to be shiny and new.

Chapter 3 Values and Care

Value Ranges

The most important factor to consider when valuing a paper collectible is the condition. Any flaws such as folds, tears, stains, etc. can significantly reduce the price of the item. We have based the value ranges in this guide to reflect books that are in mint to very good condition. A mint condition book is bright and tight, has no flaws, and looks like it just came from the publisher. In our collection we have some mint books, but they were purchased in their original mailing envelopes or were never used by their original owners. A very good condition book has no folds or tears, no stains, staples are not rusted, and the cover and pages are intact. Pictures in this guide do not always reflect very good or mint condition, but can be useful for identification.

Care of Your Collection

Once you have invested time and energy into your collection, it is important to protect your cookbooks from further aging and deterioration. We recommend that cookbooks be stored in open comic book collector bags made from virgin polypropylene which come in various sizes. Never close a cookbook in a sealed bag because the paper already contains moisture. The open bag prevents dust and allows the paper to breathe, which prevents mildew. You can also place acid-free heavyweight paper inserts in each bag to keep the book rigid and straight. Don't forget to remove any foreign paper items such as newspaper clippings or advertisements. The acid in these papers can cause a reaction in the cookbook which produces a brown stain. We must also mention the dealers who continue to put price stickers on the front covers of cookbooks and significantly reduce their value. We do not recommend removing the sticker for this could cause even further damage.

It is also important to keep your books away from direct sunlight, which deteriorates the pages and changes colors. If you wish to shelve soft cover cookbooks, we suggest a three ring binder. Simply place the cookbook wrapped in the comic bag into a three ring sheet protector and place it in a three ring notebook. To shelve hard cover books, any bookshelf with a glass cover works nicely. The objective is to keep these away from sunlight and dust; remember not to pack them too tightly. Otherwise, they rub against each other when removed and cause further wear. If you wish to display your books you can place them in stiff acrylic sleeves, often called "rigids" which come in various sizes. These supplies can easily be found at comic book stores, sports trade card stores, or in archival supply catalogs.

Chapter 4 Food Brands: Amaizo to Grennan Cakes

AMAIZO OIL

Amaizo Cook Book, 1926. American Maize-Products Company. 36 pages, 6" x 7.25". $10-$15.

ARGO CORN STARCH
(Also see Karo Syrup and Kingsford Cornstarch)

Argo Corn Starch for Delicious Desserts, ca. 1930s. 2 page leaflet, 4.5" x 6". $5-$10.

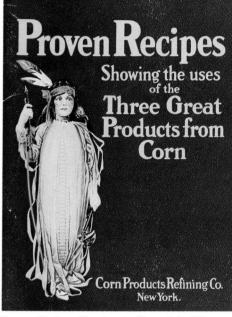

Proven Recipes Showing the Uses of the Three Great Products from Corn, ca. 1930s. 64 pages, 5" x 6.5". $15-$20.

The Modern Method of Preparing Delightful Foods, 1927. Corn Products Refining Company, hard cover. 109 pages, 4.5" x 6.75". $10-$15.

Delightful Cooking with the Three Great Products from Corn, ca. 1930s. 64 pages, 5" x 6.5". $15-$20.

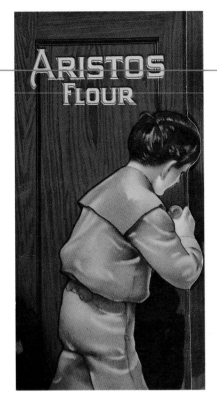

Aristos Flour, 1910. The Southwestern Milling Company. 3 page folder, 3.25" x 6.625". $15-$20.

Aristos Flour Cook Book, ca. 1911. The Southwestern Milling Company. 30 pages, 5.25" x 7.5". $15-$20.

33 Select Recipes, 1933. 12 pages, 3.25" x 6". $8-$10.

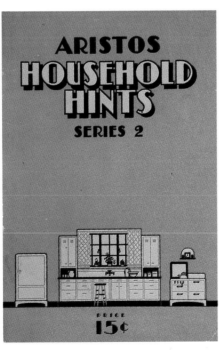

Aristos Cook Book, ca. 1911. The Southwestern Milling Company. 16 pages, 3.25" x 6.5". $25-$30.

Aristos Household Hints Series 2, ca. 1930. 34 pages, 5.25" x 7.75". $10-$15.

ARM & HAMMER BAKING SODA
(Also see Cow Brand Soda)

Arm & Hammer brand of baking soda was invented in South Hadley, Massachusetts by Dr. Austin Church in 1839. Church, a physician and part-time chemist, had been experimenting with "saleratus" or bicarbonate of soda and wanted to market the product. His brother-in-law, John Dwight, was delighted with the new business opportunity and became a partner. Hence the name John Dwight & Company.

They began manufacturing baking soda from the kitchen of Dwight's farmhouse in 1846. Eventually, the two families moved their production to New York City where they could explore new markets and expand. At this time, a third partner and investor was welcomed into the company, John R. Maurice.

Dr. Church resigned from the partnership in 1865 due to a dispute over bringing his children into the business. Although Church and Dwight remained friends, Church established his own firm and called it Church & Company.

John Dwight began selling his baking soda under the Cow Brand name in 1876, in packaging almost identical to Church's. Church patented his Arm & Hammer brand in 1878.

The companies continued to compete on the market for twenty-nine years, until 1907 when descendants of the founders decided to unite the two businesses. It was then named The Church & Dwight Company.

The familiar Arm & Hammer logo which is still used today was adopted by Church & Company. It was intended to represent the Roman god Vulcan, a blacksmith skilled in forging weapons, and was actually the idea of Dr. Church's son, James Church.

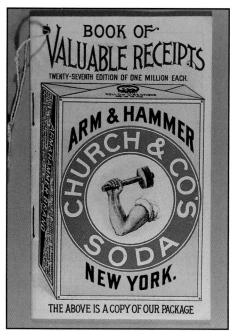

Book of Valuable Receipts, 27th Edition, 1897. 32 pages, 3.75" x 6". $30-$40.

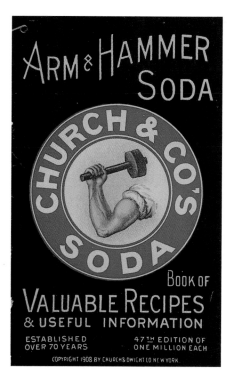

Arm & Hammer Book of Valuable Recipes, 1908. Church & Dwight Company. 32 pages, 3.5" x 5.75". $20-$25.

Arm & Hammer Soda Book of Valuable Recipes, 57th Edition, 1912. There were several editions of this cookbook for many years by Church & Dwight Company. $10-$15.

The Great Arm & Hammer Almanac, 3rd Edition, 1911. No recipes, 28 pages, 4.5" x 7". $20-$30.

A Friend in Need, 1922. No recipes, 3.5" x 5.75". $5-$10.

A Friend in Need, 1924. No recipes, 3.5"x 5.25". $5-$10.

Successful Baking for Flavor and Texture, 1934. 32 pages, 4.75" x 6.75". $5-$10.

Culinary Wrinkles, ca. 1900s. Armour and Company. 32 pages, 4" x 5". $35-$45.

Good Things to Eat, 1930. 32 pages, 3.5" x 5.75". $5-$10.

Good things to Eat, 1935. 32 pages, 3.5" x 5.75". $5-$10.

Culinary Wrinkles, ca. 1900s. Armour and Company. 32 pages, 4" x 5". $70-$85.

AUNT JEMIMA FLOUR

Aunt Jemima Pancake Flour was first developed in St. Joseph, Missouri. Two young men named Chris L. Rutt and Charles G. Underwood founded the Pearl Milling Company in 1889. Together, they developed the first self-rising pancake flour mixture on the market. After watching a vaudeville New Orleans act with the catchy tune of "Aunt Jemima," Rutt decided on a Southern mammy stereotype with a red bandanna head cover and apron. This image adorned all the flour sacks, but sales did not increase and the business soon folded.

Charles Underwood continued to pursue the endeavor with his brother, Bert, and together they formed the Aunt Jemima Manufacturing Company in 1890. Again, they were not successful and finally sold their rights to the R. T. Davis Milling Company. Mr. Davis improved the recipe by including powdered milk, so only water was needed to create the batter.

Davis obtained booth space at the 1893 Chicago World's Fair. He built the world's largest flour barrel and decorated it in a parlor-style manner so the visitors could tour inside and sample the product. Nancy Green, a talented Southern-born cook, was hired to portray the new Aunt Jemima image. She captivated the crowds with her legends, folk songs, and of course pancakes. The exhibit was an enormous success and the product became an American tradition at the breakfast table.

After the founder's death in 1900, the company went into financial ruin. Robert Clark, a former manager, reorganized the company in 1903 as the Aunt Jemima Mills Company. It continued to flourish until it was sold to The Quaker Oats Company in 1926.

Aunt Jemima's Magical Recipes, 1952. 26 pages, 4.25" x 6.25". $15-$20.

Aunt Jemima's Special Cake and Pastry Flour, 1906. Attractive die-cut recipe book, extremely rare! 40 pages, 3.5" x 5". $175-$200.

Missus - I Tole Yo dat Davis' No. 10 Flour Do Dat Way!! ca. 1890. R. T. Davis Milling Company. Pages unknown, rare, 5.5" x 8.5". $60-$75.

B & M PRODUCTS

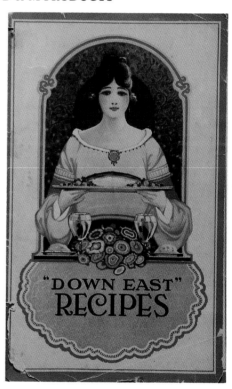

"Down East" Recipes, 1923. Written by Janet M. Hill, Burnham & Morrill Company. 28 pages, 4" x 6.75". $10-$15.

Left:
A Recipe No Other Mammy Cook Could Equal, 1930. 15 pages, 6" x 3". $60-$75.

BAKER'S CHOCOLATE

John Hannon, a young Irish immigrant, appeared in Milton, Massachusetts in 1764 and claimed he knew how to make chocolate. During that time era, chocolate had been known in Europe as a medicine to aid in digestion as well as an aphrodisiac. Chocolate was well known in the American Colonies, but there were no mills to grind chocolate beans. Dr. James Baker, from Dorchester, Massachusetts, offered to provide the necessary capital to Hannon for obtaining equipment and renting a local mill. By 1768, the business had proved to be successful and soon the operations were relocated to a larger mill in Dorchester that was owned by Baker's brother-in-law, Edward Preston. Eleven years later, in 1779, Hannon sailed off to the West Indies to buy cocoa beans and was never heard from again. He was presumed to be lost at sea.

After the business changed hands several times, Dr. Baker acquired full control of the mill in 1780 and started producing chocolate under the Baker name. The business remained family owned for over one hundred years. In 1824, the founder's grandson, Walter, renamed the business Walter Baker & Company and continued to make one of the finest confectioneries this country has ever known.

Choice Recipes by Miss Parloa and other Noted Teachers, 1904. 64 pages, 4" x 6.5". $25-$30.

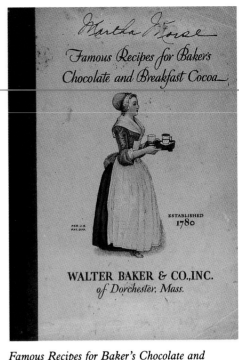

Famous Recipes for Baker's Chocolate and Breakfast Cocoa, 1928. 64 pages, 5" x 6.75". $15-$20.

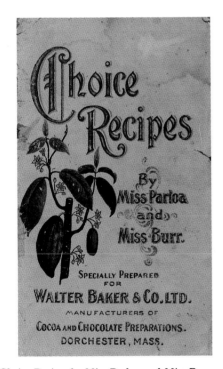

Choice Recipes by Miss Parloa and Miss Burr, 1901. 46 pages, 3.5" x 5.74". $25-$30.

Choice Recipes, 1912. Walter Baker & Company. The La Belle Chocolatie're was a portrait of Ann Baltauf painted by Jean-Etienne Liotard in 1745. Ann served Prince Ditrichstein hot chocolate at a Vienna shop and they were later married. The company chose her portrait to adorn their products and she became a well-known trademark. 64 pages, 4" x 6.5". $20-$25.

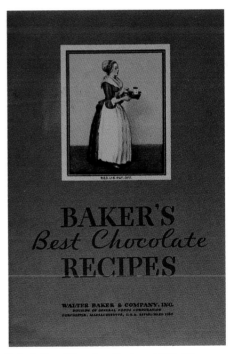

Baker's Best Chocolate Recipes, 1932. 60 pages, 4.75" x 7". $10-$15.

BAKER'S COCONUT

Franklin Baker, a flour miller from Philadelphia, was not expecting to go into the coconut business in 1895 but he was stuck with a cargo of coconuts. He had received the coconuts in exchange for a shipment of flour sent to a merchant in Havana, who was unable to raise the necessary cash for the flour. Finding it difficult to sell this produce to local markets, Baker invested in machinery and developed a method to shred the coconut meat into uniform quality. He then promoted the new product to housewives, and the gamble proved to be so successful that within two years he sold his flour mill completely! Together with his son he formed the Franklin Baker Company, moving the business to Brooklyn, New York in 1913. By 1924, both a factory and general offices were established in Hoboken, New Jersey. Baker's Coconut became part of the Postum Company in 1927.

Baker's Fresh Grated Coconut, ca. 1930s. Attractive die-cut book. 8 pages, 2.75" x 4.75". $20-$25.

Baker's Coconut Recipes, 1922. 12 pages, 4" x 6". $10-$15.

Baker's Cocoanut leaflet, ca. 1910. Note: The spelling of "cocoanut" was changed to "coconut" on Baker's items ca. 1920s. 2 page leaflet, 4" x 8". $5-$10.

Baker's Coconut Recipes, ca. 1925. 13 pages, 3.5" x 6". $15-$20.

Make It A Party with Baker's Coconut, 1927. Recipe book and calendar, nice illustrations. 16 pages, 7.5" x 5.25". $15-$20.

BAKER'S EXTRACTS

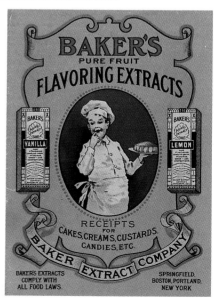

Right:
Baker's Pure Fruit Flavoring Extracts, ca. 1906. Baker Extract Company. 24 pages, 4.5" x 6". $20-$25.

BANNER BAKING POWDER

Banner Recipes, ca. 1905. Banner Baking Powder Company. 28 pages, 6" x 9". $30-$40.

BAUERLEIN BANANAS

Yes! 100 Ways to Enjoy Bananas, 1925. Bauerlein, Inc. 16 pages, 4.25" x 6". $10-$15.

Yes! Home Made Banana Recipes, 1929. Bauerlein, Inc. 24 pages, 5" x 7". $10-$15.

BEE BRAND

Bee Brand Manual of Cookery, 1927. McCormick & Company. 256 pages, 5.5" x 7.75". $15-$20.

BEECH-NUT

Beech-Nut Sliced Bacon And Other Good Things, ca. 1920s. 20 pages, 3.25" x 6". $5-$10.

BETSY ROSS BREAD

There's a Difference in Bread, 1922. The W. E. Long Company. 15 pages, 5" x 7". $10-$15.

BETTY CROCKER

During 1921, the Washburn Crosby Company, makers of Gold Medal Flour, offered the public a free flour sack pin cushion for completing a jigsaw puzzle. The response was a huge success, and many entrants asked for advice on recipes and baking solutions. Sam Gale, head of the advertising department, decided they should have a spokesperson to personally answer all the letters. Although the spokesperson would remain fictitious, the concept was created to provide a more personal contact with the homemaker. The last name was chosen as a tribute to the retired company director, William Crocker. The first name, Betty, was chosen simply because it sounded warm and friendly.

Florence Lindeberg, a worker at the mill, provided the fictitious character's first handwriting in 1921. Blanche Ingersoll became Betty Crocker's first speaking voice on the Better Crocker Cooking School, a radio program by the Washburn Crosby Company. The unveiling of the first portrait by the famous artist Neysa McMein was celebrated in June 1936, Betty's 15th anniversary.

In September 1950, the famous *Betty Crocker Picture Cookbook*, which had been in the works for ten years, was published for the General Mills Company. Over a million copies were sold the first year, breaking a new record for the publishing trade. By the 1970s, only the character's name with a large wooden spoon appeared as the company's logo. However, her reputation for quality and confidence, which graced food products for more than sixty years, will always be remembered.

New Party Cakes for All Occasions, 1933. General Mills, Inc. 24 pages, 5" x 7.25". $10-$15.

Betty Crocker Picture Cooky Book, 1948. General Mills, Inc. 44 pages, 6.25" x 9.5". $10-$15.

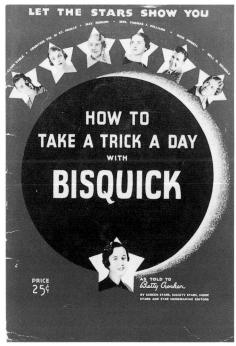

How to Take a Trick a Day with Bisquick, 1935. General Mills, Inc. This book features recipes from famous stars such as Clark Gable, Bette Davis, and Bing Crosby. 41 pages, 6.25" x 9". $15-$20.

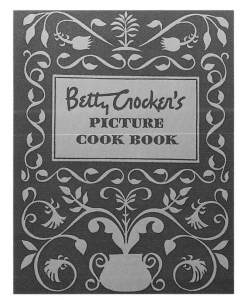

Betty Crocker's Picture Cook Book, 1950. General Mills, Inc., hard cover with five ring binder. This famous full-length picture cookbook became a national best seller and is still highly collectible today. 463 pages, 8.25" x 10.25". $40-$45.

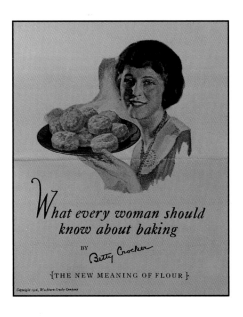

What Every Woman Should Know About Baking by Betty Crocker, 1926. Gold Medal Flour, Washburn Crosby Company. 11 pages, 5" x 6". $15-$20.

BEWLEY'S BEST

Bewley's Best Bakes Better, ca. 1920s. Bewley Mills Company. 32 pages, 4.75" x 6". $15-$20.

BLUE RIBBON MALT EXTRACT

Tested Recipes with Blue Ribbon Malt Extract, 1928. 32 pages, 5.25" x 7.75". $15-$20.

BOND BREAD

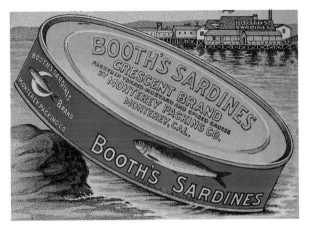

Capturing the Sunshine Vitamin in 88 New Bond Bread Recipes, 1932. General Baking Company. 32 pages, 6.55" x 4.75". $10-$15.

BOOTH'S SARDINES

Booth's Sardines, ca. 1920s. Monterey Packing Company. 14 pages, 3" x 4.5". $15-$20.

BORDEN'S MILK

Gail Borden returned from London aboard a passenger ship in 1851. Two cows that had been brought aboard to provide milk for the infants became ill. As a result, infants became sick and some even died. Borden was prompted to create a process whereby milk would stay sweet. He was successful two years later. In 1856, the first condensed milk factory opened at Wolcottville, Connecticut. Unfortunately, consumers in the East found Borden's condensed milk strange because it was pure. Up to this point, dairies used chalk for whiter color and molasses for a creamy texture. As a result, Borden went out of business.

In the spring of 1857, he was determined to try again. He re-established a working relationship with his former partners and set up in an abandoned mill at Burrville, Connecticut under the name "Gail Borden Jr. and Company." It was again destined for financial ruin. Luckily Borden had a chance meeting with a man on a train, Jeremiah Milbank, who was a grocer and banker.

Borden's Recipes, ca. 1900. Nice centerfold illustration. 24 pages, 3.5" x 8". $30-$40.

Committed solely on a handshake they became partners, and in early 1858 the New York Condensed Milk Company was created with Borden appointed President. The company flourished though they were unaware that the process of boiling the milk killed harmful bacteria resulting in lower deaths. Borden's Condensed Milk was safer than fresh milk. Borden was "pasteurizing" milk many years before Louis Pasteur introduced his discovery of microbes to the world. In 1866, Borden adopted the Eagle Brand name after some competitors put Borden's name on their inferior product.

The company's trademark, Elsie the Cow, was created in 1939 for the New York World's Fair. The public demanded to see the "real" Elsie. A Jersey cow was quickly hired and became the feature attraction of the Borden exhibit. She even had her own boudoir complete with a four-poster bed. She later made several appearances and worked on her career as Buttercup in the motion picture *Little Men*. Elsie soon became the Queen of Dairyland.

Borden's Eagle Brand Book of Recipes, ca. 1920s. Beautiful illustrations! 32 pages, 6" x 4.5". $15-$20.

New Magic in the Kitchen, 208 Delicious Dishes, ca. 1930s. 56 pages, 4.5" x 7.25". $15-$20.

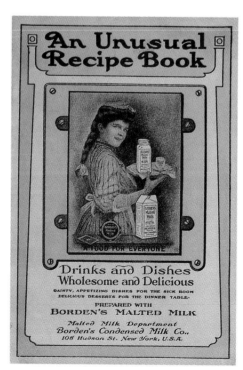

An Unusual Recipe Book, 1909. 16 pages, 4.5" x 6.5". $20-$25.

New Magic in the Kitchen, 175 Delicious Dishes, ca. 1930s. 63 pages, 4.5" x 7.25". $15-$20.

This is My Book of Magic Recipes, 1942. 22 pages, 6.5" x 8.75". $20-$25.

BRER RABBIT MOLASSES

Recipes, ca. 1930s. Penick & Ford Ltd. Inc. 3 page fold out, 3" x 6.25". $5-$10.

BUNT MARSHMALLOWS

Marshmallow Recipes, ca. 1920s. 16 pages, 4.75" x 6.25". $10-$15.

Soups, Salads and Desserts, 1916. 32 pages, 5" x 7". $25-$30.

BURT OLNEY'S PRODUCTS

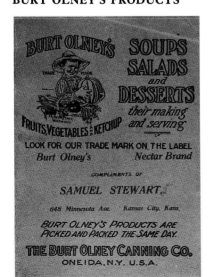

Burt Olney's Soups Salads and Desserts, 1910. 32 pages, 5" x 7". $25-$30.

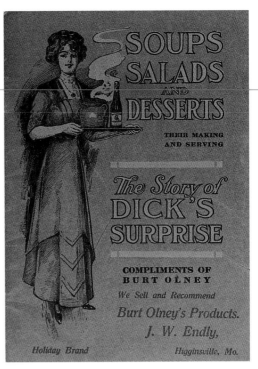

Soups, Salads and Desserts, The Story of Dick's Surprise, 1918. 24 pages, 5" x 7". $20-$25.

CALUMET BAKING POWDER

Calumet Baking Powder was invented by William W. Wright in his rented Chicago laboratory-bedroom in 1889. The product soon became so popular that he engaged the help of chemist George C. Rew to perfect the formula. By 1902, he had moved from a three story building to a successful new factory which eventually grew even larger.

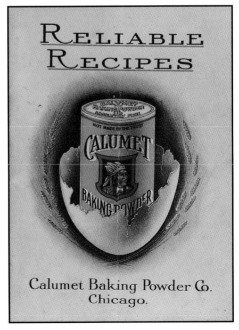

Reliable Recipes, 1909. 64 pages, 5" x 6.75". $30-$35.

Wright named his invention after the surrounding areas, such as Calumet Harbor, Calumet Lake, and the Calumet River in Chicago. The name Calumet was first used by the French as the name of a peace pipe offered to Pere Marquette when he explored the shores of Lake Michigan in 1675.

In 1928, Calumet Baking Powder Company was acquired by the Postum Company, which was forerunner to the General Foods Corporation.

Reliable Recipes, 1916. 72 pages, 4.75" x 6.75". $20-$25.

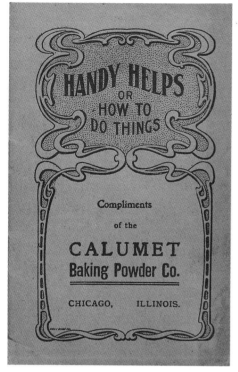

Handy Helps or How to Do Things, ca. 1909. Calumet Baking Powder Company. Advertising, no recipes. 32 pages, 3.25" x 5". $15-$20.

Twenty Lessons in Domestic Science, 1916. Marion Cole Fisher, Calumet Baking Powder, hard cover. 108 pages, 6" x 9". $20-$25.

Reliable Recipes, 1920. This book was offered free to the public, with ten cents postage pre-paid. 32 pages, 5.25" x 8.5". $15-$20.

Reliable Recipes, 1913. 64 pages, 5" x 6.75". $20-$25.

Reliable Recipes, "Always Welcome," ca. 1921. 76 pages, 5.25" x 8.75". $15-$20.

Reliable Recipes, ca. 1922. 82 pages, 5.25" x 8.5". $15-$20.

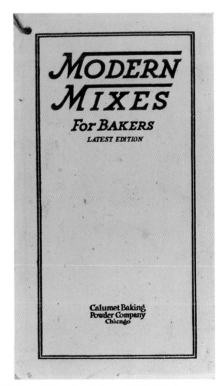

Modern Mixes for Bakers, 1922. Cloth covered board. 64 pages, 5.25" x 9". $20-$25.

Reliable Recipes, 27th Edition, 1923. 82 pages, 5.25" x 8.75". $10-$15.

A Lesson on Waffles and Griddle Cakes, 1923. 20 pages, 5" x 8". $10-$15.

Delicious Bakings Easily Prepared, ca. 1924. 6 page fold out, 3.5" x 6.25". $5-$10.

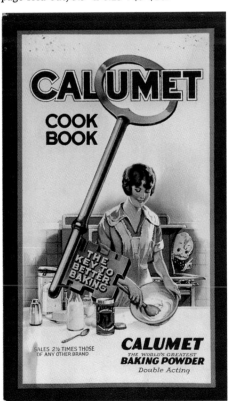

Calumet Cook Book, 1924. 84 pages, 5.25" x 8.75". $15-$20.

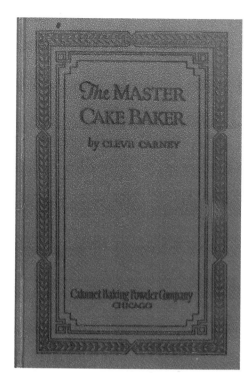

The Master Cake Baker, 1927. Cleve Carney, Calumet Baking Powder Company, hard cover. 107 pages, 6" x 9.5". $30-$35.

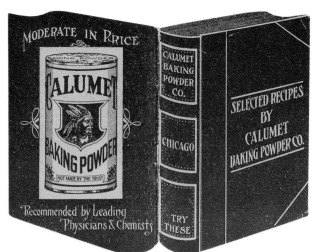

Selected Recipes by Calumet Baking Powder Company, ca. 1930s. Attractive die-cut booklet. 16 pages, 3.5" x 5.25". $25-$30.

Happy Times Recipe Book, 1934. 24 pages, 4" x 5.75". $10-$15.

The Calumet Baking Book, 89 Recipes Sure to Succeed, 1929. 32 pages, 4.75" x 6". $10-$15.

CAMPBELL'S SOUP

You would think that at the age of fifty-nine, Joseph Campbell would have been dreaming of a restful and relaxing retirement. Instead, he was dreaming of making the largest canning company in the industry. Joseph Campbell had been working with Abraham Anderson, a canner in New Jersey since 1869. Seven years later, Campbell and Anderson disagreed on the future of the business. Frustrated, Anderson told Campbell to either sell his part of the business or buy it all. Anderson was indeed surprised when Campbell chose to buy the business with a new partner, Arthur Dorrance. They named it the Jo-

Campbell's Menu Book, 1908. Joseph Campbell Company. 48 pages, 5.5" x 7.5". $30-$35.

New Edition, The Calumet Baking Book, 1930. 28 pages, 5" x 7.75". $5-$10.

seph Campbell Preserve Company in 1876.

Campbell decided that since his former partner, Anderson, had started his own business again and was now producing soup, they would do the same, but try something new. John Dorrance, Arthur's nephew, had discovered an exciting process while studying with great chefs in Europe. Based upon this discovery, the company was the first to introduce condensed soup, which had the water removed. Condensing made the soup more affordable and much easier to prepare. It was one of the first convenience foods offered to the world.

Campbell's products have been known throughout the years for those cute little chubby children featured on their advertisements and cookbooks. During 1904, the company was considering a change in their advertising to appeal to mothers through their children. A salesman of the company suggested artwork done by his wife, Grace Drayton, and soon after she was chosen to become the famous Campbell Kids artist. In 1905, the company name changed to Joseph Campbell Company and was incorporated as the Campbell Soup Company in 1923.

CAMPFIRE MARSHMALLOWS

A Book of 150 Recipes Prepared with Campfire Marshmallows, ca. 1920. 47 pages, 6" x 3.5". $10-$15.

Campfire Mal-O-Whip Summer Desserts, ca. 1920. 6 page fold out, 3.25" x 5.5". $10-$15.

CAP SHEAF SODA

The "Cap Sheaf Brand" Cook Book, ca. 1890s. DeLand & Company. 32 pages, 3.5" x 6". $15-$20.

CARNATION MILK

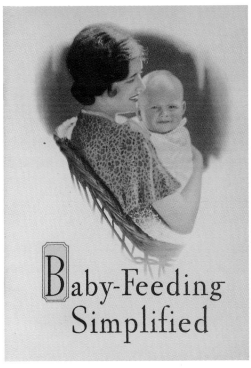

Baby-Feeding Simplified, 1930. Carnation Company. 24 pages, 5" x 7". $10-15.

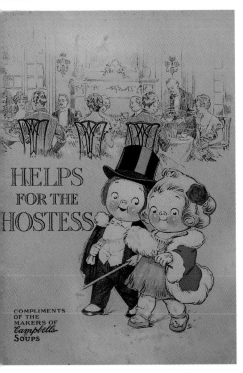

Helps For the Hostess, ca. 1910s. Joseph Campbell Company. 64 pages, 5.25" x 7.5". $30-$35.

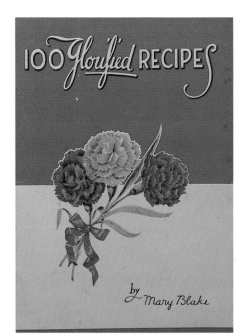

100 Glorified Recipes, 1931. Carnation Company. 36 pages, 5" x 7". $5-10.

CERESOTA FLOUR

Ceresota Flour was created by The Northwestern Consolidated Milling Company of Minneapolis, Minnesota in 1891. The new company was created by a consolidation of six Minneapolis flour millers who were distressed over the Pillsbury-Washburn flour merger that took place in 1889.

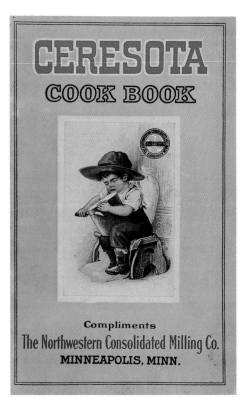

Ceresota Cook Book, ca. 1910. 32 pages, 5.5" x 8.75". $25-$30.

The product was named after the son of the Greek goddess Ce-res, pronounced "se-ries," who ruled over all harvests; Ceres Ota was her son. American advertising created the story of the boy, who travels from the heavens to explore earth. His costume is gathered from the gifts of many foreign countries. His trousers are from an Egyptian King; his blue silk blanket is from Italy; his bench, boots, suspenders, and cobweb-spun white shirt are from the Amazon; his gold shield is from Japan; and his brown sombrero is a gift from a miller and his family. The boy shows the miller how to gather and produce the most perfect flour in the world. To honor the boy, his name and a picture showing him slicing a giant loaf of bread adorned every Ceresota Flour sack product.

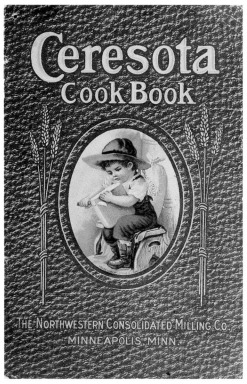

Ceresota Cook Book, 1912. 42 pages, 5" x 7.5". $25-$30.

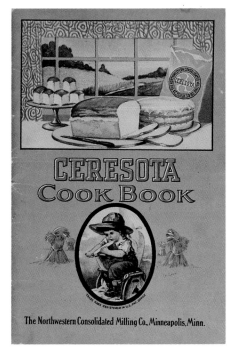

Ceresota Cook Book, ca. 1912. 32 pages, 6" x 8.75". $25-$30.

CERTO

Recipes for Making Better Jams-Jellies & Marmalades, 1926. Douglas-Pectin Corporation. 36 pages, 3.5" x 6". $5-$10.

CLABBER GIRL BAKING POWDER

Hulman Brothers began a wholesale grocery and general merchandise business in 1848 located in Terre Haute, Indiana. They developed their own brand of baking powder called Clabber in 1899. The name was chosen to represent sour milk, which was required in many earlier baking soda recipes. The product name was changed to Clabber Girl in 1923.

How to Make Jams Jellies Marmalades with One Minute's Boiling, 1927. Douglas-Pectin Corporation. 20 pages, 4.75" x 7". $10-$15.

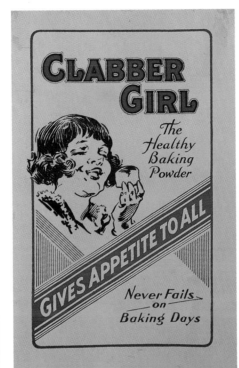

Clabber Girl The Healthy Baking Powder, 1931. 12 pages, 5.25" x 8.25". $5-$10.

Clabber Girl Baking Book, 1934. 20 pages, 5" x 7.75". $5-$10.

CONGRESS BAKING POWDER
(Also see Slade's)

Congress Cook Book, 1896. 72 pages, 4.75" x 7". $30-$35.

CHOCOLAT-MENIER

Clabber Girl Baking Book, ca. 1930s. 16 pages, 6" x 8.5". $5-$10.

Chocolat-Menier Exclusive Recipes, ca. 1915. Chocolat-Menier Company. 12 pages, 4" x 5.5". $10-$15.

COTTOLENE SHORTENING

The N. K. Fairbank Company existed from the 1880s to the 1930s. Nathanial K. Fairbank, a former grain agent, formed the company in 1880 when he opened a lard-rendering plant in Chicago, Illinois. They introduced Cottolene Shortening, which was a combination of refined cottonseed oil and beef suet. Fairbank joined with two partners, Armour and Morris, to form the American Cotton Oil Trust, making their fortune in the cottonseed market. The company not only produced Cottolene, but also manufactured Fairy Soap, Gold Dust Washing Powder, Silver Dust products, and more.

Cottolene, 1896. The N. K. Fairbank Company. Small advertising cookbook. 8 pages, 2.25" x 2.5". $40-$45.

Cottolene Twelve Telling Testimonials, ca. 1900. The N. K. Fairbank Company. 14 pages, 3" x 6". $15-$20.

Cottolene, 1893. The N. K. Fairbank Company. This book was a souvenir from the Chicago World's Columbian Exposition in 1893, where Cottolene received the gold medal. 8 pages, 3.5" x 5.5". $30-$35.

A Public Secret, 1900. Beautiful illustrations! Both the front and back covers are attractive (front cover shown at left, back cover below). 16 pages, 5" x 4". $35-$40.

Cottolene, Best for all Shortening or Frying, ca. 1910. This recipe leaflet features nice illustrations inside, as pictured unfolded below. 4 page fold out, 3.25" x 5.5". $15-$20.

COW BRAND BAKING SODA

Home Helps, A Pure Food Cook Book, 1910. This cookbook was published in both hard cover and soft cover. 80 pages, 4.75" x 7.25". $25-$35.

Dwight's Cow-Brand Cook-Book, 1895. John Dwight and Company. 32 pages, 3.5" x 5". $30-$40.

Cow Brand Soda Cook Book and Facts Worth Knowing, 1900. 33 pages, 3.625" x 5.75". $20-$30.

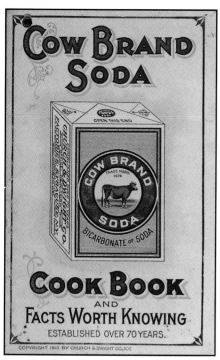

Cow Brand Soda Cook Book, 1919. Church & Dwight Company. 33 pages, 3.5" x 5.75". $10-$20.

COX GELATINE

Cox's Manual of Gelatine Cookery, 1909. 72 pages, 4.75" x 7". $15-$20.

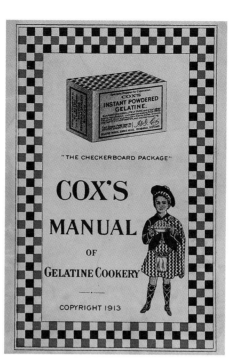

Cox's Manual of Gelatine Cookery, 1913. 64 pages, 5" x 7". $15-$20.

Cox's Gelatine Recipes, 1930. 32 pages, 4.35" x 7". $10-$15.

CREAM OF WHEAT CEREAL

The Diamond Milling Company c Grand Forks, North Dakota, had barel survived the Panic of 1893. Struggling wit. low prices and reduced demand for flou operating capital was dangerously low Tom Amidon, Head Miller, convinced th partners to start producing a new break fast porridge that his family had enjoye for some time. This porridge consisted o the unused portion of the wheat normall referred to as the "top of the steam." Hi wife would make it into a delicious dis and he called it "Cream of Wheat."

Permission was granted to pac samples with flour that was going to thei New York broker. Amidon cut the card board for the cartons by hand and labelec the packages. Wooden boxes were mad from scrap lumber. Emery Mapes, one th partners, volunteered a plate illustratio of a Black chef slinging a saucepan ove his shoulder with one hand and a steam ing bowl in the other. He chose this im age, he said, "to brighten up the package."

The mill shipped ten cases along with it regular carload of flour. Within twelve hour a telegram was received reading "Never mind shipping us anymore of your flour, but send us a carload of Cream of Wheat." The fac tory immediately switched over entirely tc production of the cereal, and by 1897 the de mand was so great they had to move. A new larger factory was developed in Minneapo lis, Minnesota under the name Cream o Wheat Company.

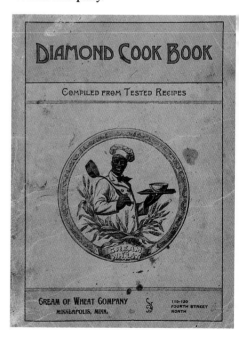

Diamond Cook Book, 1899. For a short time, a coupon was packaged in Cream of Wheat boxes. For five coupons and five cents postage, patrons received this cookbook. 156 pages, 5.5" x 7.75". $40-$50.

Crescent Baking Powder, ca. 1920. Chinese edition cookbook. 16 pages, 5.25" x 7.5". $20-$25.

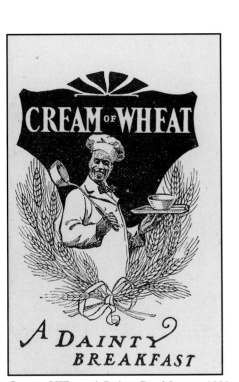

Cream of Wheat, A Dainty Breakfast, ca. 1900. 12 pages, 2.25" x 3.25". $15-$20.

Crescent Recipes, ca. 1920s. Crescent Manufacturing Company. 16 pages, 4.75" x 7.5". $5-$10.

50 Ways of Serving Cream of Wheat, 1924. 32 pages, 4.25" x 7". $35-$40.

Crisco proved to be so far advanced for its time, the company listed one of its ingredients as animal fat in order to deceive their competitors, leading them to believe it was a lard-type product. In fact, only a small percentage of fat was ever used.

Much of Crisco's success can be attributed to extensive marketing and advertising campaigns. In order to wean housewives away from the use of lard, test kitchens and cooking schools were formed. Top advertising in major magazines such as *Ladies Home Journal* in the early 1900s included ads with delicious-looking desserts and pastries. In describing its new product as "a scientific discovery that will affect every kitchen in America," Procter & Gamble's insight into the future proved to be most correct.

Crisco For Frying-For Shortening For Cake Making, 1913. Proctor & Gamble Company. 2 page leaflet, 3.25" x 6.25". $5-$10.

CRISCO SHORTENING

It was in 1907 that a German chemical engineer by the name of E.C. Kayser approached the Procter & Gamble Company with a new process of turning cottonseed oil into a pure vegetable shortening. He had invented a method of hardening the oil, thus producing a solid white substance that resembled lard but had a longer shelf life. Proctor & Gamble immediately agreed to test and manufacture the new easy-blending shortening and began production at a factory located in Macon, Georgia. The company decided to name the product "Crisco," which it thought represented purity and freshness.

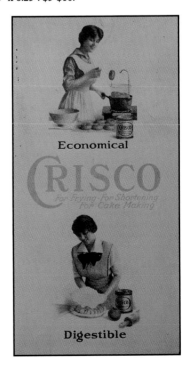

Economical

Digestible

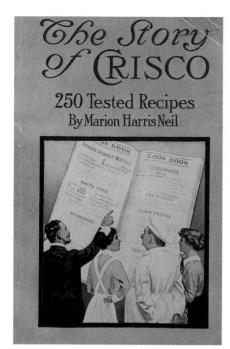

The Story of Crisco 250 Tested Recipes, 1915. Proctor & Gamble Company. Published in both hard cover and soft cover. 128 pages, 5" x 7.5". $25-$30.

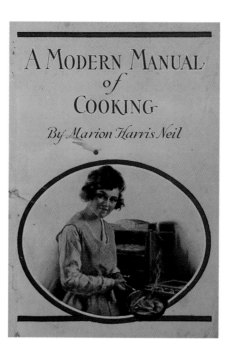

A Modern Manual of Cooking, 1921. Crisco, Proctor & Gamble Company. 128 pages, 5" x 7.25". $25-$30.

New Cooking Suggestions, 1928. Proctor & Gamble Company. 20 pages, 5" x 8". $10-$15.

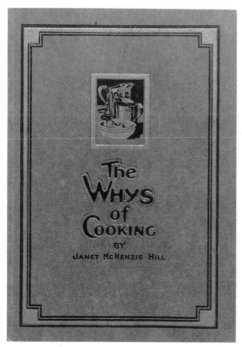

The Whys of Cooking, 1919. Janet McKenzie Hill, Crisco, The Proctor & Gamble Company. 108 pages, 5" x 7". $20-$25.

Mrs. Neil's Cooking Secrets, 1924. Crisco, Proctor & Gamble Company. 128 pages, 5" x 7.25". $25-$30.

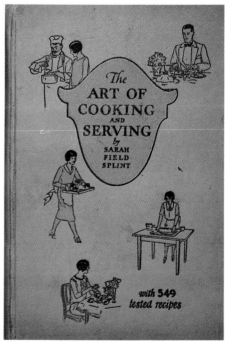

The Art of Cooking and Serving, 1930. Sarah Field Splint, Crisco Shortening, Proctor & Gamble. Hard cover. 252 pages, 5" x 7.25". $10-$15.

CURTICE BROTHERS PRODUCTS

Original Menus, 1910. Curtice Brothers Company. Each page of this *Original Menus* cookbook is filled with charming illustrations, including sample menus for picnics, yachting, and other occasions. 16 pages, 5" x 7". $40-$45.

DANIEL WEBSTER FLOUR

Daniel Webster Cook Book, 1907. Eagle Roller Mill Company. 114 pages, 5.75" x 8.75". $20-$30.

DAVIS BAKING POWDER

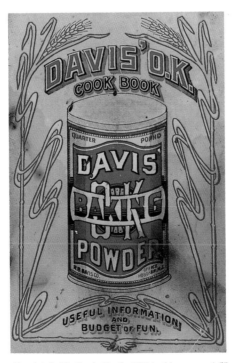

Davis' O.K. Cook Book, 1904. 64 pages, 4.5" x 7". $20-$25.

Davis Cook Book, 1904. 64 pages, 4.5" x 6.5". $20-$25.

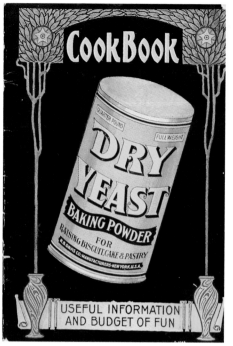

Dry Yeast Baking Powder Cook Book, ca. 1906. 64 pages, 4.5" x 6.75". $30-$35.

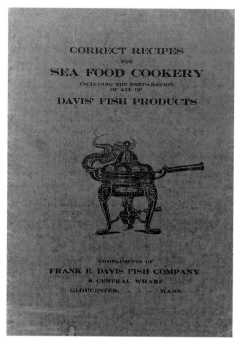

Correct Recipes for Sea Food Cookery, ca. 1900. Frank E. Davis Fish Company. 28 pages, 5" x 7". $15-$20.

DAVIS FISH

Fellow fishermen in Old Gloucester, Massachusetts laughed at Frank Davis and called him a "crank" in 1885 because he wanted to sell his fish by mail. Those fishermen didn't laugh for long. His idea to bring fresh seafood delicacies to the table of millions of homes soon turned into a thriving mail order business.

As a young boy, Davis grew up working on his father's fishing schooner. He had learned how to catch, clean, and cure fish for safekeeping. One day he sent a pail of salted mackerel to some friends. They were delighted and sent a letter of thanks and explained how difficult it was to acquire fresh fish from the ocean. With this in mind, he started sending advertising circulars into the cities offering to fill orders by express mail. Soon this entrepreneur had his own factory and turned his company into a huge success!

Sea Foods With the tang o' the sea, ca. 1930. 32 pages, 4.5" x 7". $10-$15.

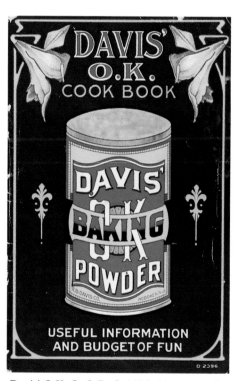

Davis' O.K. Cook Book, 1906. 64 pages, 4.5" x 6.75". $20-$25.

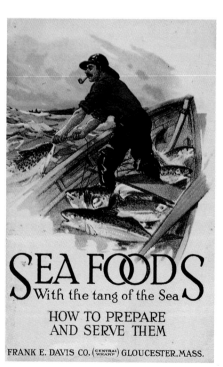

Sea Foods With the tang of the Sea, ca. 1930. 32 pages, 4.5" x 7". $10-$15.

Old Gloucester Sea Food Recipes, 1932. 32 pages, 5" x 7". $10-$15.

DAVIS FLOUR (See Aunt Jemima)

DEL MONTE FOODS

Del-Monte Recipes of Flavor, ca. 1930s. The California Packing Corporation. 62 pages, 3.25" x 6.25". $10-$15.

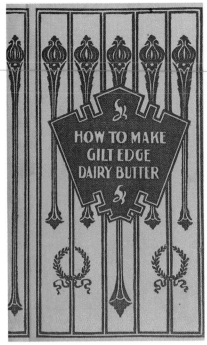

How to Make Gilt Edge Dairy Butter, 1898. Diamond Crystal Salt Company. This cookbook was published with a stiff cover and resembled a hard cover book. 20 pages, 3.5" x 5.5". $20-$25.

Del Monte Peaches, 1927. California Packing Corporation. 16 pages, 5" x 7". $10-$15.

Del Monte Tomato Sauce Recipes, 1930. The California Packing Corporation. 24 pages, 5" x 7". $5-$10.

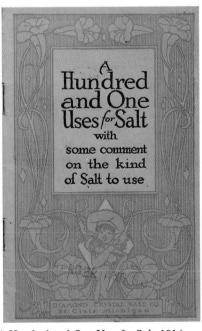

A Hundred and One Uses for Salt, 1914. Diamond Crystal Salt Company. 30 pages, 3.25" x 5". $5-$10.

DIETZEN'S BAKERY

Recipes for Sandwiches And other Appetizing Ways of Serving Bread, 1922. 16 pages, 3.5" x 6.5". $5-$10.

DILLING'S MARSHMALLOWS

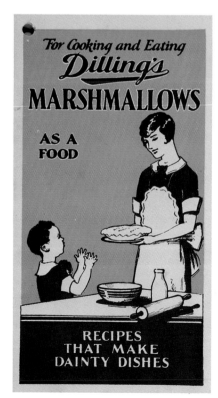

For Cooking and Eating Dilling's Marshmallows as a Food, ca. 1920. 16 pages, 3.5" x 6". $5-$10.

DOUGLAS OIL

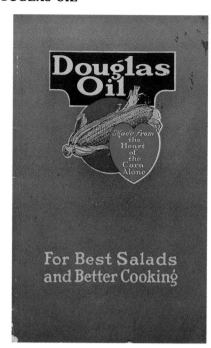

Douglas Oil For Best Salads and Better Cooking, ca. 1920s. Douglas Company. 48 pages, 5.25" x 8.5". $10-$15.

DR. PRICE'S BAKING POWDER

Delicious Desserts, 1904. 48 pages, 4.75" x 7". $15-$20.

Table and Kitchen, 1905. 61 pages, 5" x 7.25". $15-$20.

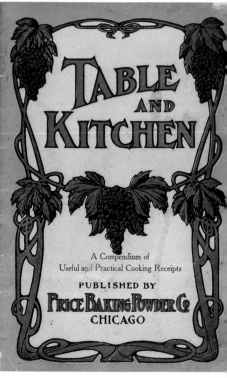

Table and Kitchen, 1909. 60 pages, 5" x 7.25". $15-$20.

36

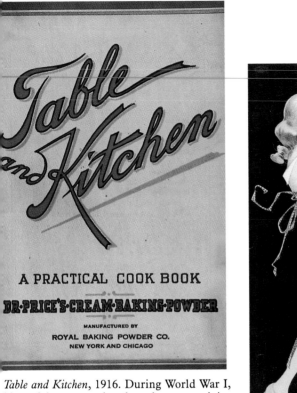

Table and Kitchen, 1916. During World War I, blue stickers were placed on the covers giving instructions for baking with less eggs. 60 pages, 4.75" x 7.25". $15-$20.

The New Dr. Price Cook Book, 1921. 50 pages, 5" x 8". $5-$10.

Foods From Sunny Lands, 1925. Dromedary Cocoanut, The Hills Brothers Company. 20 pages, 5.75" x 8.25". $15-$20.

DUFF'S MOLASSES

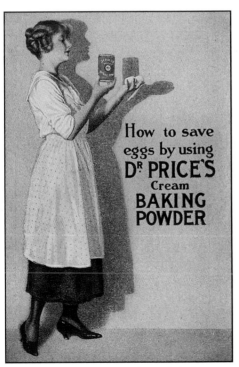

How to Save Eggs by using Dr. Price's Cream Baking Powder, 1917. 22 pages, 4.5" x 6.75". $10-$15.

Delicious Desserts and Candies, 1928. 24 pages, 5" x 7". $10-$15.

Duff's Molasses, ca. 1930s. P. Duff & Sons, Inc. 2 page folder, 3.5" x 5.75". $10-$15.

Duff's Ginger Bread Mix, ca. 1930s. P. Duff & Sons, Inc. Nice die-cut book. 16 pages, 3.5" x 4.5". $10-$15.

Duff's Bran Muffin Mix, ca. 1930s. P. Duff & Sons, Inc. Nice die-cut book. 20 pages, 3.5" x 4.5". $10-$15.

DUNHAM'S COCOANUT

Dunham's Original Shred Cocoanut, Dainty Desserts by Mrs. Sarah Tyson Rorer, ca. 1900. 32 pages, 3.5" x 6.25". $15-$20.

A Few of the Delicious Desserts made with Dunham's Original Shred Cocoanut, ca. 1900. 15 pages, 3.5" x 6". $15-$20.

DURKEE SALAD DRESSING

Salads, How to Make and Dress Them, 1907. E. R. Durkee & Company. 32 pages, 4.5" x 7.5". $15-$20.

DUTCH RUSK TEA

A Hundred Ways to Serve Hekman's Dutch Tea Rusk, 1933. Dutch Tea Rusk Company. 32 pages, 5" x 6.75". $10-$15.

EGG BAKING POWDER

Egg Baking Powder, ca. 1890s. Egg Baking Powder Company. 32 pages, 3.25" x 5.5". $35-$40. *Courtesy of James Welsh, Jr.*

FLEISCHMANN YEAST

Charles Fleischmann, an immigrant from Austria, came to the United States in the year 1863. He was very disappointed to find American bread so distasteful and inferior compared to the delicious Viennese bread in his homeland. In fact, most of the American bread during that time was made in the kitchen with fermented yeast made from potato peelings.

After returning to Austria to gather yeast samples, Fleischmann quickly returned to America with his brother, Maximilian. They approached a well-known Cincinnati, Ohio distiller named James M. Gaff with the idea to produce and market the new product. The three men formed a partnership and called it Gaff, Fleischmann & Company. By 1868, the company began making yeast in a compressed cake of uniform size that revolutionized baking.

At the Great Centennial Fair in Philadelphia in the year 1876, the brothers proudly exhibited their yeast in a extraordinary way. In a special "Vienna Bakery" display, they served guests steaming hot coffee and warm, freshly baked bread. The demand for yeast soared and larger production facilities were established.

After the death of James Gaff, around 1881, the firm's name was changed to Fleischmann and Company. By 1905, it be-

came The Fleischmann Company. On June 28, 1929, The Fleischmann Company, The Royal Baking Powder Company, and Chase & Sanborn consolidated to form Standard Brands Inc., in New York City.

Facts and Fancies, 1900. Fleischmann & Company. This is an advertising booklet, no recipes, beautiful illustrations! 12 pages, 3.25" x 4.5". $20-$25.

Fleischmann's Pure Compressed Yeast, ca. 1893. Fleischmann & Company. 2 page leaflet, 4.5" x 6.25". $15-$20.

Excellent Recipes for Baking with Fleishmann's Yeast, 1910. 52 pages, 4.75" x 6". $20-$25.

39

Good Things to Eat Made with Bread, 1913. 32 pages, 5" x 7". $15-$20.

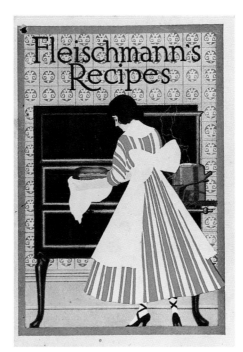

Fleischmann's Recipes, 1916. 48 pages, 4.75" x 6.75". $15-$20.

Fleischmann's Compressed Yeast and Good Health, 1919. 22 pages, 4.75" x 6.75". $15-$20.

Fleischmann's Recipes, 1914. 48 pages, 4.75" x 6.75". $15-$20.

Sixty-Five Delicious Dishes Made with Bread, 1919. 30 pages, 5" x 7". $15-$20.

Delicious Recipes, ca. 1920. 46 pages, 4" x 6.5". $15-$20.

Fleischmann's Recipes, 1920. 47 pages, 4.75" x 7". $5-$10.

Fleischmann's Recipes, 1927. 47 pages, 4.5" x 6.75". $5-$10.

FORBES SPICES

Spices How to Use them in Canning and Cooking, ca. 1928. Jas. H. Forbes Tea and Coffee Company. 16 pages, 5" x 6.75". $10-$15.

FRUIT DISPATCH COMPANY

Selected Banana Recipes, 1923. Fruit Dispatch Company. 32 pages, 4" x 8". $15-$20.

From the Tropics to Your Table, Eighty-three Tested Banana Recipes, 1926. Fruit Dispatch Company. 30 pages, 5" x 7.5". $15-$20.

GEBHARDTS CHILI POWDER

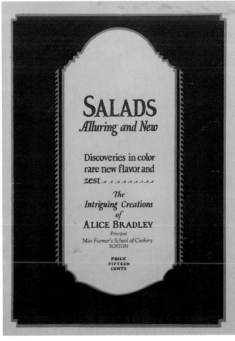

Salads Alluring and New, 1926. Gebhardts Chili Powder Company. 12 pages, 5" x 6.75". $5-$10.

GEM NUT MARGARINE

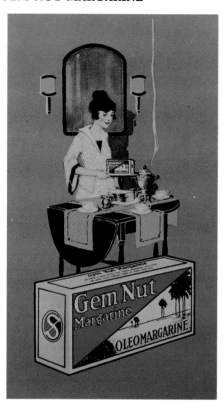

Gem Nut Margarine, ca. 1930s. Swift & Company. 4 page fold out, 3.5" x 6.25". $5-$10.

GHIRADELLI'S CHOCOLATE

Delicious Desserts, ca. 1920. 16 pages, 3.75" x 5.75". $15-$20.

Dainty Desserts, 1922. 18 pages, 3.75" x 6.25. $10-$15.

GOLD CROSS MILK

Gold Cross Evaporated Milk, 1926. Mohawk Condensed Milk Company. 16 pages, 5" x 7". $5-$10.

GOLD LABEL BAKING POWDER

Gold Label Recipes, 1925. Jaques Manufacturing Company. 16 pages, 4.75" x 6.5". $5-$10.

Delicious Desserts, 1922. 14 pages, 3.5" x 6". $10-$15.

GOLD MEDAL FLOUR

In 1866, the Washburn-Crosby Milling Company was started on the banks of the Mississippi near St. Anthony Falls in Minneapolis, Minnesota. Cadwallader C. Washburn constructed the largest flour mill in the United Sates west of Buffalo. The Washburn mill was six stories high and cost $100,000 to construct. It had the capacity to grind 840 barrels of flour daily. At first the mill was unsuccessful due to the unattractive and grayish spring wheat flour it produced. This was because the shells of the spring wheat shattered and mixed with the normal flour, creating a coarse, dark inferior flour of less value, rather than the more desired fine white soft-kernel flour. Washburn hired Edmund La Croix to build a device known as a "Middlings Purifier," which helped to produce a better grade of flour more appealing to the public.

In 1877, Washburn and John Crosby formed a new partnership and created the Washburn-Crosby Company. With new technology and the use of steel rollers they produced a high-grade wheat flour with superb qualities. They entered their three top grades of wheat in the 1880 Miller's International Exhibition in Cincinnati, Ohio and won the gold, silver, and bronze medals. In honor of the event, they named their best grade of flour "Gold Medal."

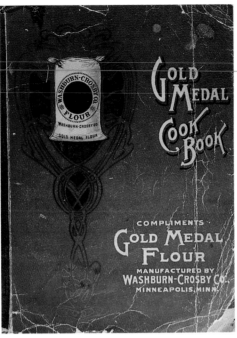

Gold Medal Cook Book, 1904. 72 pages, 8" x 10.75". $25-$30.

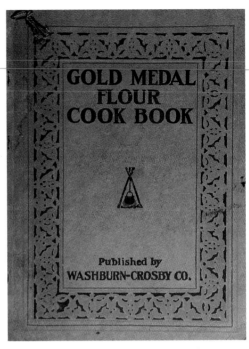

Gold Medal Flour Cook Book, 1917. This cookbook contains attractive illustrations, advertisements, and coupons in the back to send copies of the book to friends. 74 pages, 8" x 10.75". $20-$25.

Best for Every Purpose, Gold Medal Flour, ca. 1916. 8 pages, 3" x 5". $15-$20.

Washburn, Crosby Company's New Cook Book, 1894. Washburn Crosby Company. 72 pages, 8" x 11". $35-$40.

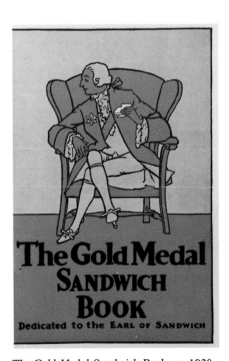

The Gold Medal Sandwich Book, ca. 1920s. Washburn Crosby Company. This book gives instructions on how to slice bread. 35 pages, 3.5" x 5.5". $10-$15.

GOLDEN GATE YEAST

Dainty Dishes How to Make Them, 1908. Golden Gate Compressed Yeast Company. 8 pages, 3" x 5.25". $15-$20.

GOOD LUCK MARGARINE

Jelke Good Luck Margarine Recipes, 1922. John F. Jelke Company. 36 pages, 5" x 7". $10-$12.

GRANDMA'S OLD FASHIONED MOLASSES

Grandma's Old Fashioned Molasses Recipes, 1927. 30 pages, 5.5" x 7.5". $5-$10.

GOLDEN RULE PRODUCTS

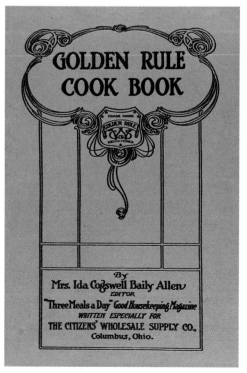

Golden Rule Cook Book, 1916. The Citizens Wholesale Supply Company. 130 pages, 6" x 9". $20-$30.

Recipes, Jelke Good Luck Margarine, 1927. 40 pages, 5" x 7". $10-$15.

GRENNEN CAKES

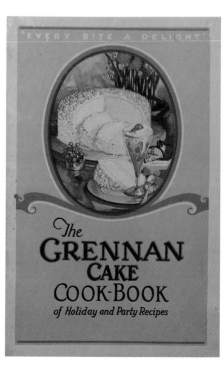

The Grennan Cake Cook-Book, 1928. Grennan Bakeries, Inc. Nice illustrations. 22 pages, 5.5" x 8.5". $10-$15.

HAWAIIAN PINEAPPLE

Ninety-Nine Tempting Pineapple Treats, 1924. Association of Hawaiian Pineapple Canners. 32 pages, 3.25" x 6.25". $5-$10.

Hawaiian Pineapple as 100 Good Cooks Serve It, 1927. Association of Hawaiian Pineapple Canners. 32 pages, 3.25" x 6.25". $5-$10.

HEBE MILK

Hebe Recipes and Menus by Noted Authorities on Home Cooking, ca. 1920s. 20 pages, 5" x 7". $10-$15.

HECKERS' FLOUR

Heckers' Self-Rising Superlative Flour was invented by John and George Hecker of New York City in 1852. After ten years of production at the Croton Flour Mill, which they had built in 1843, the local millers decided to add a leavening agent to their flour, making it the first "self-rising" product of its kind. It was advertised "For making most delicious White Wholesome and Light Bread, Biscuit and Best of Cake and Pastry."

HEINZ FOODS

Henry John Heinz had employed three women to work tending his garden and was making trips in a wagon to Pittsburgh selling vegetables before the age of sixteen. By the time he was almost thirty, he entered into a partnership with L. C. Noble in 1869 and started the Heinz Noble and Company. Their main product was horseradish, however they went bankrupt during the panic of 1875. Henry wasn't the type of man to give up easily. Being bankrupt, he couldn't hold shares of another company for many years.

Salads By The Worlds Best Chefs, 1912. H. J. Heinz Company. 24 pages, 3.5" x 6". $30-$35.

Heckers' Household Recipes, ca. 1881. Geo. V. Hecker Company, Croton Flour Mills. Beautiful illustrations. 16 pages, 4" x 6.75". $45-$55.

So he formed a second company, F. & J. Heinz in 1876, with his brother John and cousin Fredrick. This company prospered mainly due to the production of ketchup, pickles, and other condiments. Twelve years later, Henry reorganized the company when his debt was clear and renamed the company after himself, H. J. Heinz, in 1888. Henry was also responsible for thinking up the slogan "57 Varieties," which wasn't really the total number of products, but rather what he thought sounded good. The slogan obviously worked and Heinz products have become a common household name. Tasty Heinz Ketchup can be found on almost every restaurant table across America.

Heinz Book of Salads, 1925. H. J. Heinz Company. 90 pages, 4.5" x 7.5". $20-$25.

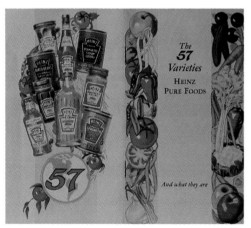

The 57 Varieties Heinz Pure Foods, ca. 1925. H. J. Heinz Company. 12 pages, 3.5" x 6". $10-$15.

HELLMANN'S MAYONNAISE

German immigrant Richard Hellmann first introduced mayonnaise to America. He came to the United States in 1903 and opened a delicatessen in New York City two years later. His wife had made several versions of mayonnaise to serve on salads and sandwiches, however one "blue ribbon" formula was far more popular. He proudly displayed a jar with a blue ribbon tied around it on the counter of the store. By 1912, Richard Hellmann's Blue Ribbon Mayonnaise was being packaged and sold in labeled jars and by 1913 delivery by truck was available. The product soon became so successful that in 1915 he built his first manufacturing factory in the Astoria area of Queens, in New York. He incorporated his business as Richard Hellmann's Inc. the following year. In 1927, Hellmann merged with the Postum Company, which later became the General Foods Corporation. The recipe has basically remained the same over the years.

Correct Salads for All Occasions, 1931. General Foods Corporation. 30 pages, 5" x 6.75". $5-$10.

The Chef's Standby, 1922. John Behrmann, Inc. 12 pages, 3.5" x 5.5". $5-$10.

Richard Hellmann's Blue Ribbon Mayonnaise, 1925. This unusual, die-cut recipe book with calendar and dial is difficult to find completely intact. Often, the unattached cookbook is mistakenly sold by itself. Richard Hellman, Inc. 20 pages, 4.5" x 10". $50-$55.

HERSHEY'S CHOCOLATE

It has been said that Milton Snavely Hershey "built a town on a cake of chocolate" in 1903. Hershey was born in 1857. His father wanted him to become a printer, his mother insisted on an industrial trade, and he eventually apprenticed with a candy maker for four years. At the age of nineteen he opened his own candy shop. Six years later it failed and he went to work for a caramel manufacturer in Denver, Colorado. In 1886, Hershey returned to Lancaster, Pennsylvania and established the Lancaster Caramel Company, which he sold in 1900 for one million dollars. Hershey always had a dream of mass-producing chocolate at a low price. In 1905, he proceeded to build The Hershey Chocolate Company factory in Derry Church, Pennsylvania. The five-cent Hershey Chocolate Bar was a huge success, and the town of Derry Church was soon renamed Hershey, Pennsylvania. He generously helped build schools, a community center, a stadium, and a medical center, and gave loans to employees to build their own homes. Hershey was so generous to the community that before his death he donated the entire company to a school for orphaned children he and his wife had established near the factory. His vision of a thriving company nestled in the fertile Lebanon Valley of the Blue Ridge Mountains not only produced one of the best model towns in the United States, but one of the most affordable delicious desserts this country has ever known.

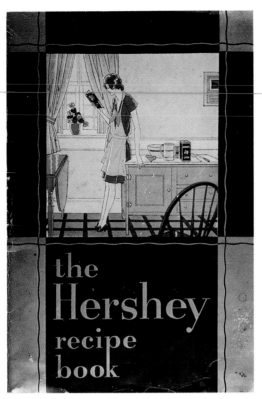

The Hershey Recipe Book, 1930. 80 pages, 6" x 9". $15-$20.

Hershey's Recipes, 1940. 32 pages, 4.75" x 6.5". $15-$20.

A Cookery Expert's New Recipes, ca. 1915. 12 pages, 5.5" x 8". $15-$20.

Hershey's Index Recipe Book, 1934. Illustrated by Frances Tipton Hunter (1896-1957), who also illustrated for Calumet Baking Powder. 48 pages, 5.5" x 7.5". $20-$25.

HILLS BROTHERS COFFEE
(Also see Dromedary)

Excellent Topping for Many Desserts, Recipes,
1940. 12 pages, 2.75" x 4.75". $5-$10.

Cultivation and Preparation of Coffee and Tea,
1922. Hills Brothers. 28 pages, 5" x 7". $10-$15.

HIRES' ROOT BEER

How to Make Delicious Wholesome Hires Beverages, 1935. The Charles E. Hires Company. 8 page fold out, 3" x 4.25". $15-$20.

HOLSUM BREAD

In 1916, the W.E. Long Company was responsible for more modern marketing practices by wrapping each loaf of bread in a dust-tight sanitary package. This created a more healthful condition of delivery, instead of the traditional unwrapped loaves in wagons which were exposed to dust and insects. It was at this time that William Edgar Long, President, introduced the product called Holsum Bread.

Hershey's Recipes, 1949. 32 pages, 4.5" x 6.5". $5-$10.

How Things Have Changed Since Mother was a Girl, 1916. W. E. Long Company. 24 pages, 4.75" x 7.75". $15-$20.

Toast and It's Various Uses, 1924. W. E. Long Company. 14 pages, 6" x 7.5". $5-$10.

HOOD'S SARSAPARILLA

Charles I. Hood moved from Vermont to Lowell, Massachusetts in 1861. There he began his apprenticeship under a druggist by the name of Theodore Metcalf and Company of Boston. By 1870, the enterprising Hood had formed a partnership with a friend from Lowell and opened his own drugstore. Six years later he was the sole owner and began making his medicines and selling them in his store as well as nearby towns.

Under the Hood's label, he nationally advertised such products as Hood's Sarsaparilla, a popular health drink of the 1800s, and Hood's Pills. His creative marketing ideas consisted of almanacs, calendars, coupons, trade cards, posters, and even jigsaw puzzles. All of his advertising was highly illustrated with cherubic children's faces or attractive female images, always including wit and humor to capture attention.

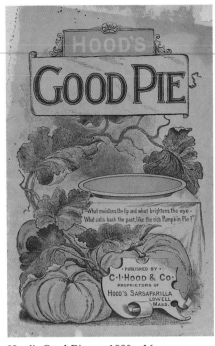

Hood's Good Pie, ca. 1880s. 16 pages, 4.75" x 7". $20-$25.

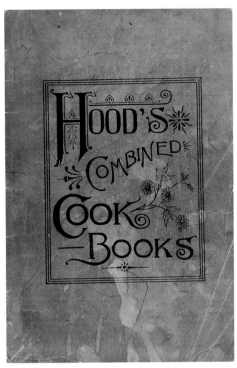

Hood's Combined Cook Books, ca. 1880s. 110 pages, 5" x 7.5". $30-$35.

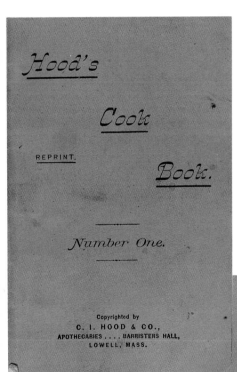

Good Bread, The Staff of Life, ca. 1880s. 16 pages, 4.75" x 7.25". $20-$25.

Hood's Cook Book Number One, 1877. C. I. Hood & Company. This is thought to be the first known cookbook from Hood's. The pictures above and right show the front and back covers. 4.5"x7". $30-$35.

HORSFORD BAKING POWDER
(Also see Rumford Baking Powder)

Hood's Book of Home Made Candies, 1888. C. I. Hood & Company, Ltd. 16 pages, 4.75" x 7". $20-$25.

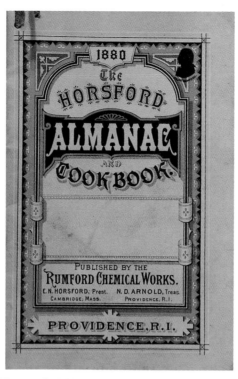

The Horsford Almanac and Cookbook, 1880. Rumford Chemical Works. 48 pages, 4.75" x 7". $50-$60. *Courtesy of Nick and Nancy DeShetler.*

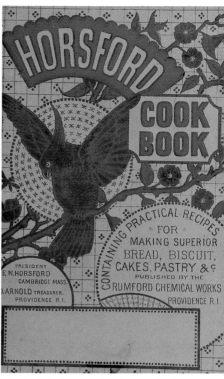

Horsford Cook Book, 1881. Rumford Chemical Works. 48 pages, 4.75" x 7". $40-$50. *Courtesy of Nick and Nancy DeShetler.*

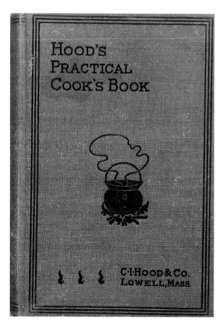

Hood's Practical Cook's Book, 1897. C. I. Hood & Company, hard cover. 351 pages, 4.5" x 6". $50-$65.

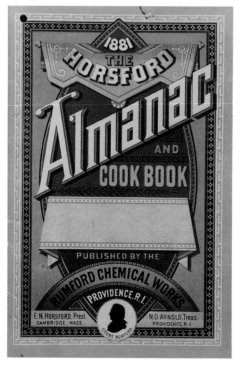

The Horsford Almanac and Cookbook, 1881. Rumford Chemical Works. 48 pages, 4.75" x 7". $50-$60.

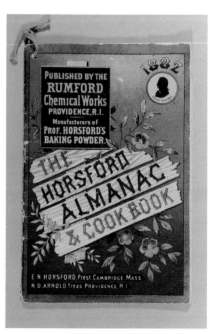

The Horsford Almanac & Cook Book, 1882. Rumford Chemical Works. 48 pages, 4.75" x 7". $45-$55. *Courtesy of Nick and Nancy DeShetler.*

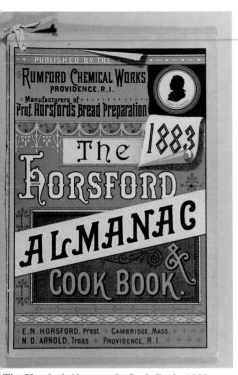

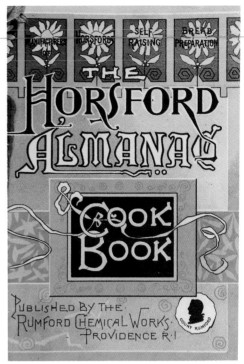

The Horsford Almanac & Cook Book, 1883. Rumford Chemical Works. 48 pages, 4.75" x 7". $45-$50. *Courtesy of Nick and Nancy DeShetler.*

The Horsford Almanac and Cook Book, 1885. Rumford Chemical Works. 36 pages, 4.75" x 7". $45-$55. *Courtesy of Nick and Nancy DeShetler.*

The Horsford Almanac and Cook Book, 1887. Rumford Chemical Works. 30 pages, 4.75" x 7". $45-$55. *Courtesy of Nick and Nancy DeShetler.*

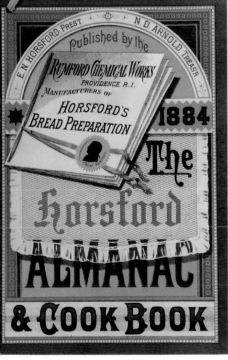

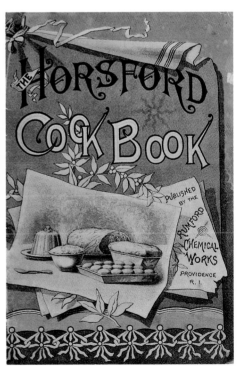

The Horsford Almanac & Cook Book, 1884. Rumford Chemical Works. 36 pages, 4.75" x 7". $45-$55. *Courtesy of Nick and Nancy DeShetler.*

The Horsford Almanac and Cook Book, 1886. Rumford Chemical Works. 36 pages, 4.75" x 7". $45-$55. *Courtesy of Nick and Nancy DeShetler.*

The Horsford Cook Book, ca. 1887. Rumford Chemical Works. 36 pages, 4.75" x 7". $40-$45. *Courtesy of Nick and Nancy DeShetler.*

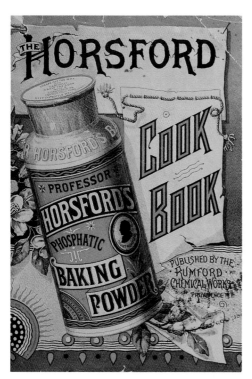

Horsford Cook Book, ca. 1887. Rumford Chemical Works. 36 pages, 4.75" x 7". $50-$55. *Courtesy of Nick and Nancy DeShetler.*

The New Horsford's Bread and Pastry Cook, ca. 1890. Rumford Chemical Works. 48 pages, 4" x 6.5". $25-$30. *Courtesy of Nick and Nancy DeShetler.*

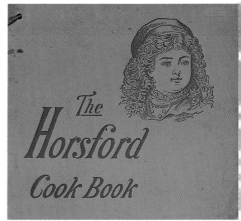

The Horsford Cook Book, ca. 1891. Rumford Chemical Works. 24 pages, 5" x 4.5". $20-$25. *Courtesy of Nick and Nancy DeShetler.*

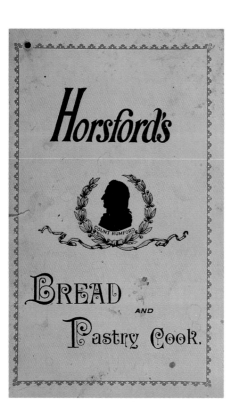

Horsford's Bread and Pastry Cook, ca. 1890. Rumford Chemical Works. 48 pages, 3.5" x 5.75". $25-$30. *Courtesy of Nick and Nancy DeShetler.*

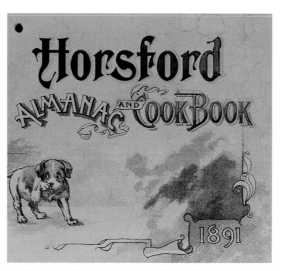

Horsford Almanac and Cook Book, 1891. Rumford Chemical Works. 34 pages, 4.75" x 4.5". $40-$45. *Courtesy of Nick and Nancy DeShetler.*

Horsford's Acid Phosphate, ca. 1922. Rumford Chemical Works. Illustrated by John Bradshaw Crandell. 8 pages, 3.5" x 6.25". $25-$30.

A WHOLESOME TONIC
HORSFORD'S ACID PHOSPHATE
(Non-Alcoholic)

Horsford's Acid Phosphate, ca. 1922. Rumford Chemical Works. 8 pages, 3.5" x 6.25". $25-$30. *Courtesy of Nick and Nancy DeShetler.*

HUNT'S BAKING POWDER

Hunt's Perfect Baking Powder, 1908. Hunt's Perfect Baking Powder Company. 40 pages, 4" x 6.75". $10-$15.

JACK FROST BAKING POWDER

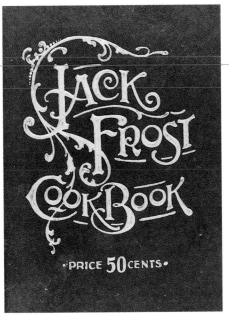

Jack Frost Cook Book, ca. 1930s. F. B. Chamberlain Company. 76 pages, 5" x 6.75". $20-$25.

JELL-O

You wouldn't think that a man who dropped out of school at the age of twelve, and couldn't hold a steady job, would turn out to be the owner of a million dollar company. Orator Francis Woodward, owner of the Genesee Pure Food Company, purchased the failing Jell-O product from Pearl B. Wait in LeRoy, New York in 1897. Woodward was anxious to introduce this new product to the world. However, during the early 1900s, the common desserts were rich cakes and pies. People simply were not interested in a translucent dessert. After two years of hardship, Woodward offered the whole business to his factory superintendent for $35 but he refused the offer. Woodward had no choice but to continue to promote the product.

Woodward invested in an advertisement in *The Ladies Home Journal* featuring fashionably dressed ladies wearing clean white aprons and enthusiastic smiles, with the slogan "America's Most Famous Desert." Following the advertisement was a massive postal distribution of free samples, along with beautifully illustrated recipe booklets. Famous artists were commissioned, such as Maxfield Parrish, Norman Rockwell, and Rose O'Neill, who were always in high demand.

The "Jell-O Girl" was a famous symbol of America's Favorite Dessert. She was actually Elizabeth King, the four-year-old daughter of an advertising executive hired by Woodward. She helped contribute to Jell-O's success by promoting a product which was easy to prepare and pleasing to children.

In 1925, Woodward changed the name to The Jell-O Company. The public was greatly attracted to these recipe booklets when they were first distributed, and collectors continue to consider them highly prized items even today.

Jell-0, 1904. The Genesee Pure Food Company. One of the first publications, rare. 12 pages, 3.5" x 6.25". $100-$125.

Jell-0 Ice Cream Powder, "So Easy to Prepare," 1904. The Genesee Pure Food Company. One of the first Jell-O Ice Cream Powder publications, rare. 12 pages, 3.5" x 6.25". $80-$100.

Jell-0 The Dainty Dessert, 1905. The Genesee Pure Food Company. 12 pages, 3.5" x 6". $65-$75.

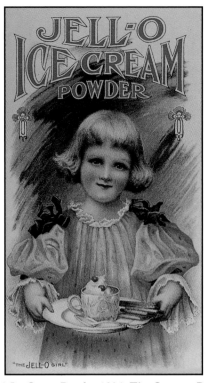

Jell-0 Ice Cream Powder, 1906. The Genesee Pure Food Company. 12 pages, 3.25" x 6". $65-$75.

Jell-0 Ice Cream Powder Makes Ice Cream Sherbets Ices Puddings, ca. 1906. The Genesee Pure Food Company. 10 pages, 4.5" x 6.25". $65-$75.

Jell-0 Ice Cream Powder, 1905. The Genesee Pure Food Company. 16 pages, 3" x 5". $50-$60.

Jell-0 The Dainty Dessert, ca. 1906. The Genesee Pure Food Company. 8 pages, 3.25" x 6". $60-$70.

Jell-0 Ice Cream Powder Makes Ice Cream, Sherbets, Ices and Puddings, 1907. The Genesee Pure Food Company. 12 pages, 4" x 5.5". $65-$75.

They Wanted Jell-0, 1909. The Genesee Pure Food Company. This is an unsigned Rose O'Neill. 12 pages, 4.5" x 4.5". $65-$75.

Hello? Jell-0 The Dainty Dessert, ca. 1910. The Genesee Pure Food Company. 8 pages, 4.5" x 4.5". $60-$70.

Jell-0 "Yes. Jell-O, please all seven flavors," 1912-13. The Genesee Pure Food Company. This book was also published with a similar cover that had an orange background. 14 pages, 4.25" x 6". $40-$50.

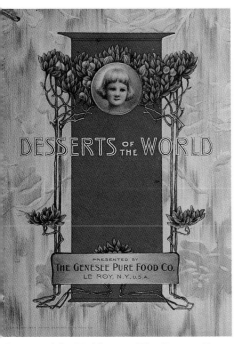

Desserts of the World, 1909. The Genesee Pure Food Company. This is an unsigned Rose O'Neill, exquisite illustrations. 20 pages, 5.25" x 7.25". $75-$85.

What Six Famous Cooks Say of Jell-O, 1912. The Genesee Pure Food Company. 12 pages, 4.5" x 6.25". $40-$50.

Jell-0 "Even if you can't cook you can make a Jell-O dessert," 1913. The Genesee Pure Food Company. 12 pages, 4.5" x 6.25". $40-$50.

The Jell-O Girl Entertains, 1914. The Genesee Pure Food Company. 16 pages, 5.25" x 7". $60-$70.

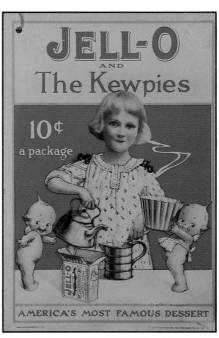

Jell-0 and The Kewpies, 1915. The Genesee Pure Food Company. 18 pages, 4.25" x 6.25". $70-$80.

All Doors Open to Jell-0, 1917. The Genesee Pure Food Company. This recipe booklet was printed with and without the price of two boxes in the right-hand corner. 18 pages, 4.25" x 6.25". $35-$45.

The Jell-0 Girl Gives a Party, 1914. The Genesee Pure Food Company. 16 pages, 5.25" x 7". $55-$65.

Jell-0 America's Most Favorite Dessert, 1916. The Genesee Pure Food Company. This book provides the new bride with recipes and prepares her for unexpected guests. 18 pages, 4.25" x 6.25". $40-$50.

New Talks About Jell-0, 1918. The Genesee Pure Food Company. This recipe booklet was printed with and without the price of two boxes in the right-hand corner. 14 pages, 4.25" x 6.25". $25-$35.

Many Reasons for Jell-0, 1920. The Genesee Pure Food Company. 14 pages, 4.25" x 6.25". $15-$20.

"It's So Simple" Jell-0, 1922-23. The Genesee Pure Food Company. Illustrated by Norman Rockwell (1894-1978). 14 pages, 4.25" x 6.25". $20-$25.

Jell-0 Rhymes, 1923. The Genesee Pure Food Company. Illustrated by Lucile Patterson Marsh. 20 pages, 4.25" x 6.25". $25-$35.

For Economy Use Jell-0, 1920. The Genesee Pure Food Company. 14 pages, 4.25" x 6.25". $15-$20.

Jell-O Ice Cream Powder Makes Ice Cream, Ices, and Puddings, 1923. Rare. 4 pages, 4.25" x 6.25". $30-$35. *Courtesy of James Welsh, Jr.*

1924 A Jell-0 Year, 1924. The Genesee Pure Food Company. Illustrated by Lucile Patterson Marsh. 14 pages, 4.25" x 6.25". $25-$35.

Polly Put The Kettle On We'll All Make Jell-0, 1924. The Genesee Pure Food Company. Illustrated by Maxfield Parrish. 18 pages, 6.25" x 4.25". $65-$75.

Jell-0 Train Scene, 1924. The Genesee Pure Food Company. This recipe book was published with a vertical and horizontal cover. 18 pages, 4.25" x 6.25". $15-$20.

Jell-0 America's Most Favorite Dessert, 1926. The Genesee Pure Food Company. 18 pages, 6" x 4.25". $15-$20.

The Charm of Jell-0, 1924. The Genesee Pure Food Company. 32 pages, 5.5" x 8.25". $20-$25.

Jell-0 Ice Cream Powder, 1925. The Genesee Pure Food Company. 6 pages, 4.25" x 6.25". $20-$25.

ELLYCON GELATINE

Burnham's Jellycon, ca. 1890s. E. S. Burnham Company. 8 pages, 3.5" x 6". $40-$45.

JENNY WREN FLOUR

Jenny Wren Recipes, 1926. Jenny Wren Company. 12 page fold out, 3" x 5". $5-$10.

Jenny Wren Recipes, 1926. Jenny Wren Company. 15 pages, 5" x 6.75". $10-$15.

JUNKET GELATINE

England had been enjoying the delicate dish commonly called curds and whey or "Devonshire Junket" for hundreds of years. History does not record the exact person who discovered that ferment or enzyme rennet when added to milk transforms it into a custard form, but it was Christian D. Hansen who was responsible for introducing the rennet extract to the world.

Dainty Delicacies for Artistic Desserts, 1897. Chr. Hansen's Laboratory. Indicates this is the first cookbook made for Junket. 32 pages, 3.25" x 2.5". $35-$45.

The Christen D. Hansen's Laboratory was established in Copenhagen, Denmark in 1874. Hansen developed a liquid commercial version of the rennet extract and called the product Junket. When added to milk and flavoring, it made a healthful and delicious pudding-like dessert. Shortly after the Centennial Exposition in Philadelphia in 1876, the American demand for Junket became so great that a laboratory was established in Little Falls, New York. Its popularity continued, winning hundreds of awards including the first prize medal for Junket Tablets at the World's Columbian Exposition in Chicago in 1893.

Dainty Junkets, 1913. 32 pages, 3" x 2.75". $20-$25.

Have Some Junket! 1917. 32 pages, 3" x 2.75". $20-$25.

Delicious Desserts and Milk Foods made with Junket, 1923. 22 pages, 4.25" x 6.25". $20-$25.

Delicious Quick Desserts, 1929. 24 pages, 5" x 7.25". $10-$15.

How to Make Delicious Rennet-Custards and Smooth Ice Cream, 1936. 26 pages, 5.25" x 7.75". $10-$15.

Junket Recipes, 1926. 18 pages, 4.25" x 6.25". $10-$15.

A Century of Progress in Junket, 1933. This was a souvenir from the Century of Progress International Exposition during the Chicago World's Fair. 4 page fold out, 4.5" x 6". $10-$15.

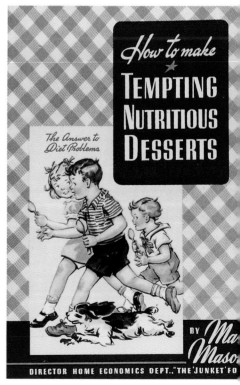

How to Make Tempting Nutritious Desserts, 1941. 30 pages, 5.25" x 7.75". $10-$15.

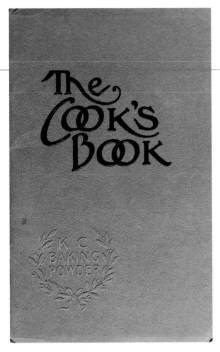

New Recipes, ca. 1911. 16 pages, 3.25" x 6". $5-$10.

Favorite Recipes from the K C Baking Powder Cook's Book, ca. 1920s. 6 page fold out, 3" x 6.25". $5-$10.

The Cook's Book, 1909. Front cover shown above. This is the first inside page which gives an example of the nice illustrations throughout. Jaques Mfg. Co. 60 pages, 4.75" x 7.5". $20-$25.

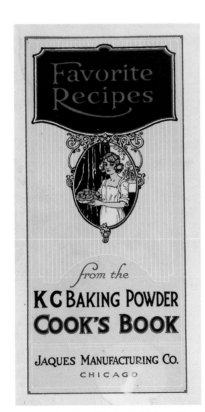

Favorite Recipe from The K C Baking Powder Cook's Book, ca. 1920s. 6 page fold out, 3" x 6.25". $5-$10.

Favorite Recipes from the K C Baking Powder Cook's Book, ca. 1920s. 6 page fold out, 3" x 6.25". $5-$10.

Favorite Recipes from the K C Baking Powder Cook's Book, ca. 1920s. 6 page fold out, 3" x 6.25". $5-$10.

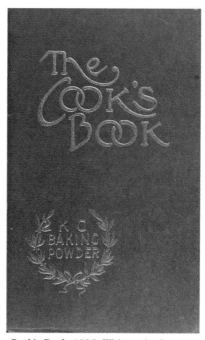

The Cook's Book, 1935. Written by Janet McKenzie Hill. 48 pages, 4.75" x 7.75". $15-$20.

Preserve With Karo and Be Assured of Perfect Results, 1912. Corn Products Refining Company. 12 pages, 3.5" x 6.25". $15-$20.

KARO SYRUP
(Also see Argo Cornstarch and Kingsford Cornstarch)

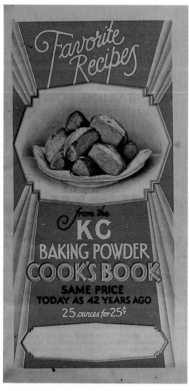

Favorite Recipes from the K C Baking Powder Cook's Book, ca. 1920s. 6 page fold out, 3" x 6.25". $5-$10.

Karo Cook Book, 1910. Corn Products Refining Company. The illustration on this book was done by Joseph Christian Leyendecker (1874-1951). He became well known after his first cover design in 1899, and illustrated over 300 advertising pieces. 47 pages, 5" x 6.5". $15-$20.

Corn Products Cook Book, ca. 1912. Corn Products Refining Company. 40 pages, 4.5" x 6.25". $15-$20.

In 1898, Will Keith Kellogg experimented with a flake cereal. It consisted of boiled corn meal mush that was run through metal rollers. It was originally introduced as a health food item with his brother, Dr. John Kellogg, at his sanitarium located in Battle Creek, Michigan.

In 1906, Will Kellogg broke away from his brother John and created the Battle Creek Toasted Corn Flake Company. His corn flakes were packaged under the name Sanitas Toasted Corn Flakes. He later changed the product name to Kellogg Toasted Corn Flakes. It was a good idea since the name Sanitas meant disinfectant and didn't help sales.

The next year Will Kellogg renamed the company the Toasted Corn Flake Company. Two years later he changed the name again to the Kellogg Toasted Corn Flake Company. His brother, Dr. John Kellogg, had renamed *his* company the Kellogg Food Company, which distributed products with the same types of slogans and packaging. Will Kellogg sued his brother John Kellogg for the rights to the family name and finally won in 1921.

Corn Products Cook Book, ca. 1912. Corn Products Refining Company. 40 pages, 4.5" x 6.25". $15-$20.

New Suggestions for Serving Karo, ca. 1933. Corn Products Sales Company. 2 page leaflet, 4.5" x 6". $5-$10.

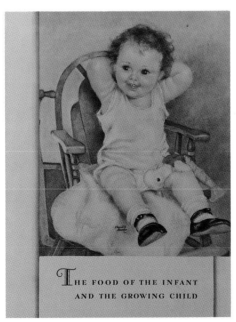

The New Karo Maple, ca. 1915. Corn Products Refining Company. 2 page leaflet, 4" x 6". $10-$15.

The Food of the Infant and the Growing Child, 1934. Corn Products Refining Company. 16 pages, 6.25" x 8.25". $15-$20.

A Breakfast Food Rich in Vitamin "B," ca. 1905. ZO Breakfast Food. The Battle Creek Food Company. 2 page leaflet, 3.5" x 6.25". $5-$10.

Healthful Living, ca. 1926. The Battle Creek Food Company. 64 pages, 6" x 8.75". $10-$15.

Keep on the Sunny Side of Life, 1933. Kellogg Company. 32 pages, 5.25" x 7.25". $5-$10.

King's Dehydrated Fruits and Vegetables, ca. 1915. Kings Food Products Company. Attractive die-cut book. 24 pages, 4.5" x 6.5". $20-$25.

Three Meals A Day, 1928. Kellogg Company. 20 pages, 4" x 8". $5-$10.

The Sunny Side of Life Book, 1934. Kellogg Company. 32 pages, 5.25" x 7.25". $5-$10.

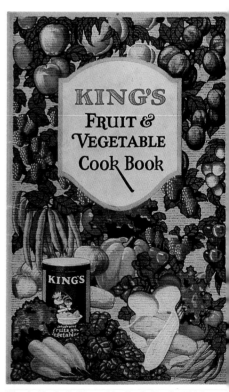

King's Fruit & Vegetable Cook Book, 1922. King's Food Products. 64 pages, 5" x 7.75". $10-$15.

KINGSFORD CORNSTARCH
(Also see Karo Syrup and Argo Cornstarch)

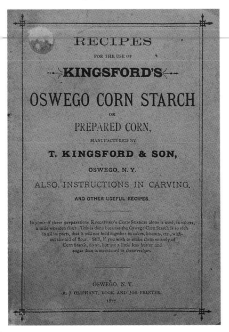

Recipes For the Use of Kingsford's Oswego Corn Starch, 1877. 64 pages, 4.25" x 6.25". $25-$30.

What a Cook Ought to Know about Corn Starch, 1909. 47 pages, 5" x 6.5". $15-$20.

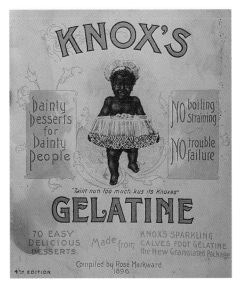

Knox's Gelatine, 1896. Charles B. Knox. This book was compiled by Mr. Knox's wife, Rose Markward. 32 pages, 5.25" x 6". $30-$40.

Original Recipes and Cooking Helps, 1907. 48 pages, 5" x 6.5". $15-$20.

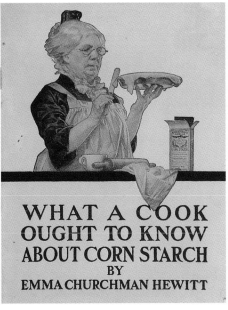

What a Cook Ought to Know about Corn Starch, 1910. 47 pages, 5" x 6.5". $15-$20.

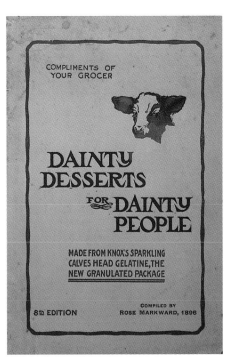

Dainty Desserts for Dainty People, 1896. C. B. Knox. 31 pages, 4.5" x 6.5". $20-$25.

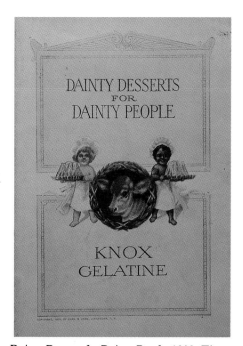

Dainty Desserts for Dainty People, 1909. The Chas. B. Knox Gelatine Company, Inc. 36 pages, 5" x 7". $20-$25.

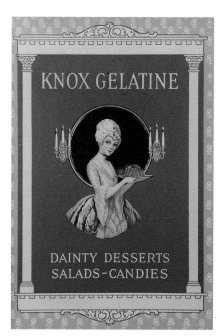

Knox Gelatine, Dainty Desserts Salads-Candies, 1927. 46 pages. 4.5" x 6.75". $15-$20.

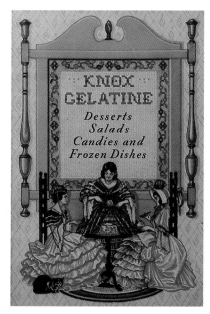

Knox Gelatine Desserts Salads Candies and Frozen Dishes, 1941. 55 pages, 4.25" x 6.5". $10-$15.

KRAFT CHEESE

James L. Kraft, the son of a Canadian farmer, was very determined to start his own profession in 1903. With a horse and wagon he had purchased for sixty-five dollars, he started a wholesale cheese distribution business in Chicago. Kraft hoped to relieve the grocers of their daily trip to the wholesale district by delivering and selling cheese to their door. The business failed the first year and Kraft lost his initial investment, as well as his horse.

Cheese and Ways to Serve It, ca. 1920. 32 pages, 4.75" x 7". $10-$15.

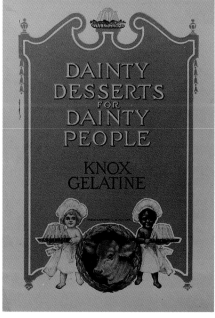

Dainty Desserts for Dainty People, 1924. The Chas. B. Knox Gelatine Company, Inc. 41 pages, 4.75" x 6.75". $15-$20.

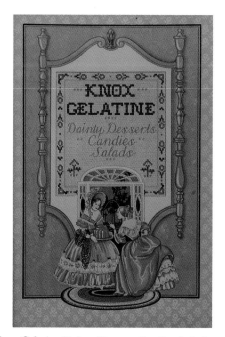

Knox Gelatine Dainty Desserts Candies Salads, 1929. 47 pages, 4.5" x 6.75". $10-$15.

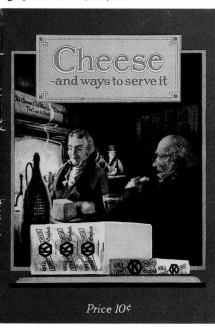

In 1909, Kraft and his four brothers joined in partnership and incorporated as the Kraft & Bros. Company. Through hard work and determination the business was advertising and selling thirty-one varieties of cheese under the name Kraft and Elkhorn by 1914, with a factory established in Illinois.

Perhaps the most innovative idea with which the company will always be associated is the development of blended, pasteurized cheese. Before refrigeration, cheese was sold in wheels and was subject to deterioration soon after opening. In 1915, Kraft invented a method of blending and heating cheese resulting in a uniform flavor, longer shelf life, and convenient packaging. He received a patent in 1916 and it was one of the most successful products of its kind.

KREAM KRISP SHORTENING

Kream Krisp The Universal Shortening, 1917. Berlin Mills Company. 23 pages, 3.25" x 6". $10-$15.

LARABEE'S FLOUR

Kitchen Magic with Little Princess Flour, ca. 1920s. 8 page fold out, 3.5" x 7". $10-$15.

Kitchen Magic with Larabee's Best Flour, ca. 1920s. 8 page fold out, 3.75" x 6". $10-$15.

Cheese And Ways to Serve It, ca. 1923. J. L. Kraft & Brothers. 32 pages, 5" x 7". $10-$15.

Tempting Salads with Wright's Mayonnaise, ca. 1930. 3 page die-cut fold out, 3.25" x 5.75". $5-$10.

Larabee's Recipes, ca. 1920s. 32 pages, 3" x 5". $10-$15.

LARKIN PRODUCTS

Larabee's Best Flour, 1931. 8 page fold out, 4.75" x 7". $15-$20.

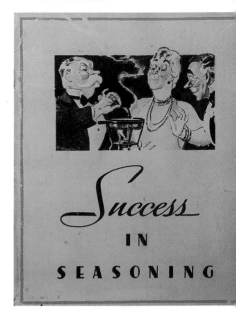

Good Things to Eat And How to Prepare Them, 1909. Larkin Company, cloth cover. 71 pages, 5" x 7.75". $10-$15.

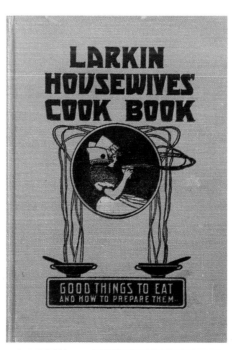

Dolly Madison Hostess, ca. 1930s. 34 pages, 4.5" x 6". $15-$20.

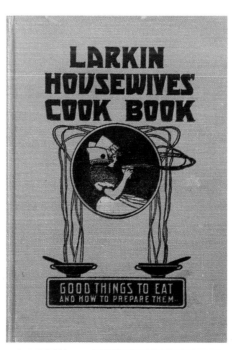

Larkin Housewives' Cook Book, 1923. Larkin Company, Inc., hard cover. 140 pages, 5.75" x 8". $15-$20.

LEA & PERRINS

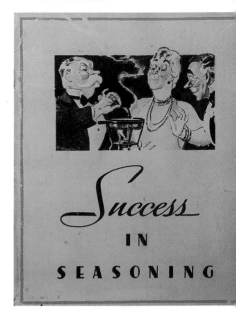

Success in Seasoning, 1934. Lea & Perrins, Inc. 48 pages, 6" x 7". $10-$15.

LOG CABIN SYRUP

The demand for a more economical maple-flavored syrup is what prompted Patrick J. Towle, a Chicago grocer, to create his famous Log Cabin Syrup in the 1880s.

Log Cabin Recipes, 1906. Towle's Maple Syrup Company. 32 pages, 3.5" x 6". $30-$35.

Towle experimented until he found the best blend of sugar cane with Vermont and Canadian syrup. He began selling the product in his grocery store. After sales escalated, he moved to St. Paul, Minnesota where he established the Towle Maple Syrup Company in 1887.

Ten years later, he began selling his syrup in cabin-shaped tin containers which became the symbol of his company for many years. The idea was created from his admiration for President Lincoln and his boyhood cabin home. The empty tins were a favorite toy among children and remain highly collectible today. The business later changed its name to The Log Cabin Products Company and was purchased in 1927 by the Postum Company.

The Towle name was also applied to other products, such as Towle's Bucket Syrup and Towle's Circus Syrup. These brands were made by the Pioneer Maple Products Company. The Towle family apparently manufactured these products after the sale of their former company to Postum.

Towle's Bucket Syrup, ca. 1930s. The Pioneer Maple Products Company. Attractive die-cut. 2 page leaflet, 3" x 3.5". $15-$20

LOWNEY'S CHOCOLATE

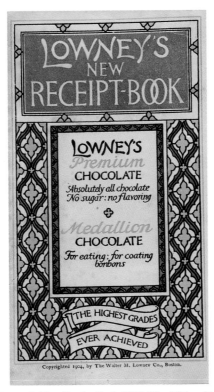

Lowney's New Receipt-Book, 1904. The Walter M. Lowney Company. 36 pages, 3.5" x 6.25". $20-$25.

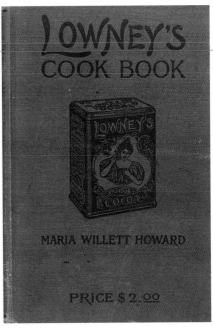

Lowney's Cook Book, 1907. Maria Willett Howard, Walter M. Lowney Company, hard cover. 421 pages, 5.5" x 8". $20-$25.

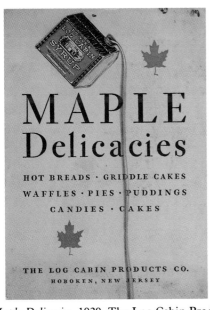

Maple Delicacies, 1929. The Log Cabin Products Company, General Foods Corporation. 12 pages, 5" x 7". $20-$25

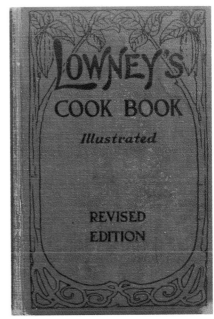

Lowney's Cook Book, 1912. Maria Willett Howard, Walter M. Lowney Company, hard cover, color illustrations. 421 pages, 5.5" x 8". $20-$25.

Log Cabin Syrup Recipes, ca. 1930s. General Foods Corporation. Attractive die-cut book. 14 pages, 4.5" x 3.75". $25-$35

Chapter 6 Food Brands: Maid-Rite to Ryzon

MACA YEAST
(See Yeast Foam)

MADE-RITE FLOUR

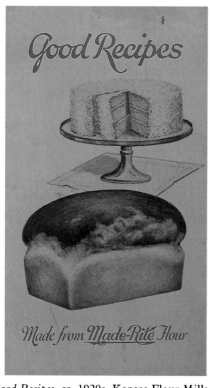

Good Recipes, ca. 1920s. Kansas Flour Mills Corporation. 2 page leaflet, 3.5" x 6.25". $5-$10.

MAGIC YEAST
(See Yeast Foam)

MALTA-VITA CEREAL

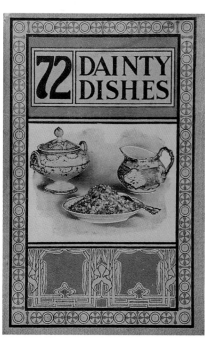

MAPLEADE SYRUP

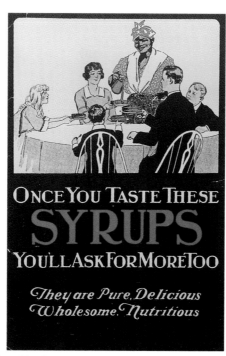

Once You Taste These Syrups You'll Ask For More Too, ca. 1930s. W. B. Roddenbery. 3 page fold out, 4" x 6". $15-$20.

MAPLEINE EXTRACTS

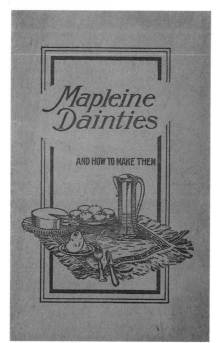

Mapleine Dainties How to Make Them, ca. 1910s. Crescent Manufacturing Company. 16 pages, 3.25" x 5.25". $5-$10.

72 Dainty Dishes, 1898. Compiled by Edna Kenderdine Hatch. Company is not identified. 32 pages, 3.25" x 5". $15-$20.

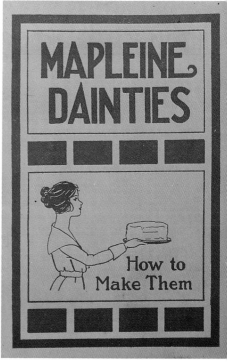

Mapleine Dainties How to Make Them, ca. 1910s. Crescent Manufacturing Company. 16 pages, 3.25" x 5.25". $5-$10.

Mapleine Dainties How to Make Them, ca. 1910s. Crescent Manufacturing Company. 16 pages, 3.25" x 5". $5-$10.

Mapleine Cookery, ca. 1920s. Crescent Manufacturing Company. 32 pages, 5.25" x 7.5". $10-$15.

MAZOLA OIL
(Also see Karo Syrup and Argo Cornstarch)

The Corn Products Company was begun in 1906 by E. T. Bedford in Argo, Illinois. Mazola Corn Oil was produced in 1911 as a side product from the Corn Products Refining Company. It was first packaged in a can with the illustration of an Indian woman with a corn cob body. Mazola 100% corn oil remains the leading selling corn oil in the United States and Germany today.

Mazola Recipes, ca. 1915. Corn Products Refining Company. 24 pages, 4.5" x 6.5". $15-$20.

MEADOW GROVE CREAM CHEESE

Genuine Meadow Grove Brand Full Cream Cheese, ca. 1920s. Meadow Grove Company. 30 pages, 6" x 8". $10-$15.

MID-CENTRAL FISH COMPANY

Fish and Seafood Cookery, ca. 1930s. Mid-Central Fish Company. 32 pages, 5.5" x 8.5". $5-$10.

MINUTE TAPIOCA/GELATINE

In 1894, Susan Stavers of Boston, Massachusetts was nursing a sick friend back to health in her home. One evening she decided to serve him tapioca pudding for dessert. The young sailor was not impressed. Susan, proud of her reputation for good home cooking, prodded the young man until he finally told her the truth. He did not like her tapioca because it was "too lumpy." Surprised at his answer, she then asked "I suppose you know how to make it without lumps?" "Yes," he replied. "All you have to do is just grind the tapioca flakes in your coffee grinder!"

Susan took his suggestion, and her smooth and delectable tapioca dessert was so popular she began packing it in paper bags and selling it throughout the community.

When John Whitman, owner of a local newspaper, heard of her success, he bought the rights from Stavers and started the Whitman Grocery Company to sell the product. He first named it Tapioca Superlative, but later changed it to Minute Tapioca in admiration of the famed Minute Men of the Revolutionary War. He also added the famous symbol of the Minute Man, which is still in use today.

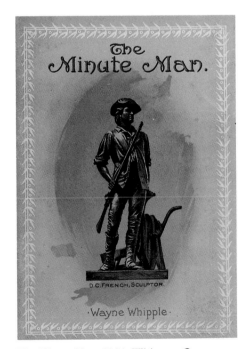

The Minute Man, 1904. Whitman Grocery Company. Wonderful illustrations! 30 pages, 5" x 7". $20-$25.

The Best is the Cheapest. The Leading and Popular Dessert, 1908. Minute Tapioca Company. This is actually two books combined in one. The reverse is a Minute Gelatine cookbook. 20 pages, 2.5" x 4.25". $20-$25.

A Few Minute Tapioca and Minute Gelatine Recipes, ca. 1910. Minute Tapioca Company. 6 page fold out, 3.5" x 6.25". $10-$15.

Adding Variety to The Menu, 1925. 16 pages, 4.75" x 7.25". $10-$15.

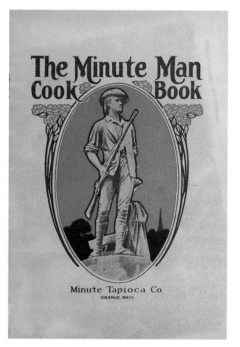

The Minute Man Cook Book, 1909. Minute Tapioca Company. 34 pages, 5" x 7". $15-$20.

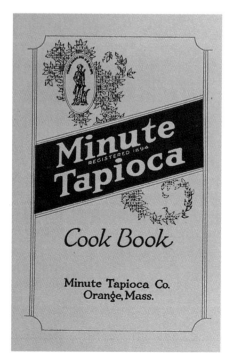

Minute Tapioca Cook Book, 1922. Minute Tapioca Company. 16 pages, 4.5" x 7". $15-$20.

30 New Recipes From the $20,000 Cook Book, 1929. 22 pages, 4.75" x 4.75". $10-$15.

MORRELL'S PRODUCTS

Morrell's Pride Book on Hospitality, 1922. Written by Ida Bailey Allen, John Morrell & Company. 36 pages, 5.25" x 8". $5-$10.

Meat Curing Made Easy, 1934. Morton Salt Company. 40 pages, 8.5" x 11". $10-$15.

Housekeeping Wisdom, ca. 1900. 16 pages, 4.25" x 8". $10-$15.

MORTON SALT

MURDOCK PRODUCTS

The Story of Salt, 1933. Morton Salt Company, no recipes. 20 pages, 8.5" x 11". $10-$15.

Murdock's Cook Book, ca. 1890s. 32 pages, 3.5" x 6". $20-$25.

Dainty Dishes, ca. 1905. 16 pages, 6" x 4.75". $10-$15.

NATIONAL LIVE STOCK

Meat for the Family, 147 Meat Recipes, 1925. National Live Stock and Meat Board. 48 pages, 4.75" x 7.75". $10-$15.

NATIONAL YEAST

National Yeast, 1885. National Yeast Company. 44 pages, 3.5" x 6.25". $35-$40.

Dainty Dishes, ca. 1910. 16 pages, 4.5" x 6". $10-$15.

MY-T-FINE PRODUCTS

Meat for the Family, 155 Meat Recipes, 1925. National Live Stock and Meat Board. 48 pages, 4.75" x 7.75". $15-$20.

NESTLE

Nestle's Lion Brand Milk Evaporated, ca. 1925. Nestle's Food Company. 2 page leaflet, 3.5" x 6.5". $5-$10.

More! Good Things to Eat Prepared With MY-T-FINE Quality Food Products, ca. 1929. My-T-Fine Corporation. 3 page fold out, 3.25" x 6". $5-$10.

NONE SUCH MINCE MEAT

Good Pies - Easy to Make, ca. 1920. Merrell-
Soule Company. 24 pages, 5.5" x 8.75".
$5-$10.

OLD GRIST MILL WHEAT FLOUR

Old Grist Mill Health Food Preparations, ca.
1890s. Potter & Wrightington. 8 pages, 3.5" x
5.25". $15-$20.

OLD MANSE MOLASSES

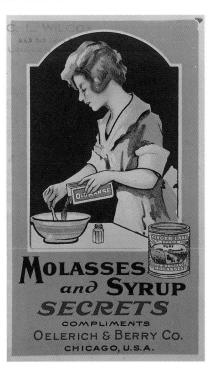

Molasses and Syrup Secrets, ca. 1920s. Oelerich
& Berry Company. 14 pages, 3.5" x 6". $5-$10.

OMEGA FLOUR

Omega Flour Tested Recipes, ca. 1930s. Omega
Flour Mills. 24 pages, 4" x 6". $15-$20.

ONION SALT SEASONING

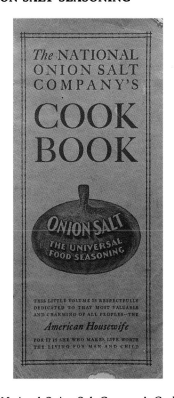

*The National Onion Salt Company's Cook
Book*, 1911. The National Onion Salt Company. 15 pages, 4" x 9". $15-$20.

NORSE CROWN PRODUCTS

*Norse Crown Seafood Products and Fifty Ways
to Serve Them*, 1924. Norse Crown Canning
Company, Inc. 15 pages, 4.5" x 7". $5-$10.

ORIENTAL "SHOW-YOU" PRODUCTS

Oriental "Show-You" Recipes, ca. 1930s. Oriental Show-You Company. 3 page fold out, 4.5" x 7". $10-$15.

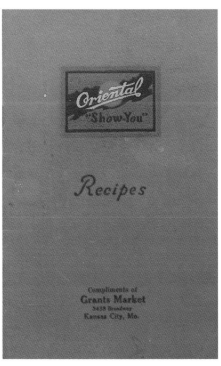

Oriental "Show-You" Recipes, ca. 1930s. Oriental Show-You Company. 24 pages, 4.5" x 7". $10-$15.

PENICK SYRUP

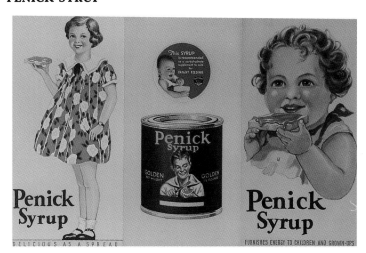

Penick Syrup, ca. 1930s. Penick & Ford Ltd. Inc. 3 page fold out, 3" x 6.25". $10-$15.

PENNANT SYRUP

Pennant Recipes for Tempting Foods, ca. 1930s. Union Starch and Refining Company. 23 pages, 3.25" x 6.25". $5-$10.

PERFECTION PRODUCTS

Perfection Cook Book, ca. 1930s. The California Perfume Company. This company was the predecessor to Avon Products. David H. McConnell started selling perfumes, toilet articles, and flavoring extracts door-to-door. The name was changed to Avon in 1939. 23 pages, 3.5" x 6.25". $5-$10.

Perfection Recipe Book, ca. 1940s. Avon Products, Inc. 23 pages, 3.5" x 6.25". $5-$10.

PET MILK

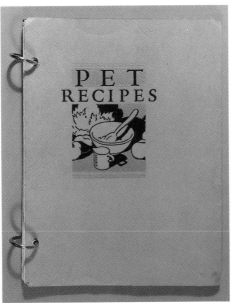

Pet Milk Frozen Desserts, 1925. Pet Milk Company. Illustrated by William Andrew Loomis (1892-1959), who had a long career in advertising illustration as well as editorial design. 12 pages, 4.5" x 6". $15-$20.

Pet Milk Cook Book, 1923. Pet Milk Company. Illustrated by Norman Price (1877-1951), who was well known for his historical illustrations. 36 pages, 5" x 7.5". $20-$25.

Pet Recipes, 1930. Pet Milk Company. 80 pages, 6.5" x 8.5". $10-$15.

PILLSBURY FLOUR

After working at his uncle's hardware supply business in Minneapolis, Minnesota, twenty-seven-year-old Charles A. Pillsbury decided to make a career change. He bought one-third of a local flour mill on the banks of the Mississippi river and started the Pillsbury Company in 1869. Pillsbury's improvements and state-of-the-art milling machinery led the successful entrepreneur to purchase six more mills by 1889 and he continued to build it into the famous industry it is today.

The famous trademark, "Pillsbury's Best XXXX," had its origins with the Christian era. Early millers had used the symbol "XXX" to symbolize bread after the death of Christ. Each "X" represented the crosses on Calvary and medieval millers used the mark for quality on their flour. Pillsbury added the fourth "X" to prove that Pillsbury's flour was the very best and printed it on every sack.

"Pillsbury Vitos," The Ideal Breakfast Food, 1898. 4 pages, 3.5" x 6.25". $25-$30.

A Book for a Cook, 1905. 128 pages, 5.5" x 8.75". $45-$50.

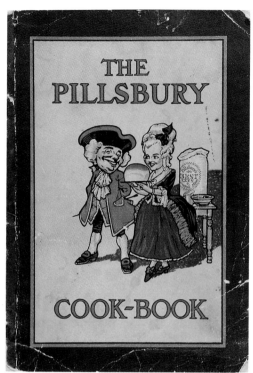

The Pillsbury Cook-Book, 1914. 126 pages, 6.5" x 9.25". $30-$35.

100 Delicious Foods from 4 Basic Recipes, 1923. 30 pages, 5.25" x 6.25". $15-$20.

Your Family's Food, Pillsbury's Family of Foods, 1922. 10 pages, 3.5" x 6". $10-$15.

The Pillsbury Cook Book Illustrated, 1911. This book included a pass for a free tour of the mill. 126 pages, 6.5" x 9.5". $25-$30.

Pillsbury's Cook Book, 1921. Beautiful advertisements and illustrations. 96 pages, 8" x 10". $35-$40.

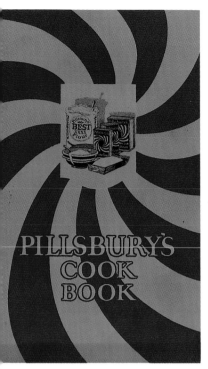

Pillsbury's Cook Book, 1929. 48 pages, 5" 8". $10-$15.

PILLSBURY GRAND NATIONAL CONTESTS "BAKE-OFFS"

The first Grand National Recipes and Baking Contest was held in 1949 by Pillsbury in New York City's Waldorf-Astoria Hotel. Contestants developed new recipes to use with specific products and winners received expensive prizes, publicity, and had their recipes published. Planned as only a one-time event, it was so successful the company continued it each year and "Bake-Offs" became an American tradition.

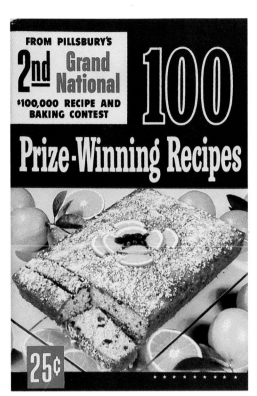

100 Prize Winning Recipes, 2nd Grand National, 1951. 100 pages, 6" x 9". $10-$15.

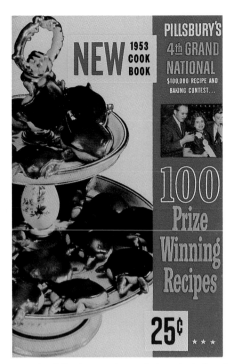

100 Prize Winning Recipes, 4th Grand National, 1953. 96 pages, 6" x 9". $10-$15.

100 Prize Winning Recipes, 3rd Grand National, 1952. 96 pages, 6" x 9". $10-$15.

100 Prize Winning Recipes, 1950. This was the first in a series of Grand National Recipe Contests, the first contest starting in 1949. The first is considered rare. 96 pages, 6" x 9". $55-$65.

PIONEER SALT

Pioneer Salt and Its Many Uses, ca. 1920s. Carey Salt Company. 22 pages, 3.25" x 5". $5-$10.

The Story of Plymouth Rock, 1901. The Plymouth Rock Gelatine Company. Beautiful illustrations. 40 pages, 5.25" x 7.5". $25-$30.

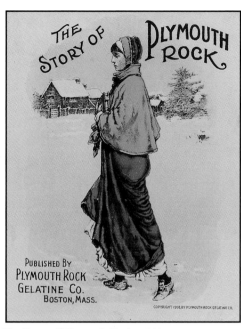

The Story of Plymouth Rock, 1908. 10 pages, 4" x 5.25". $10-$15.

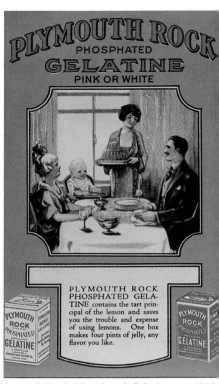

Plymouth Rock Phosphated Gelatine, ca. 1910. 2 page leaflet, 3.5" x 5.5". $10-$15.

POSTUM CEREAL

Plymouth Rock Gelatine Dainties and Household Helps, ca. 1908. 8 pages, 4.5" x 6". $15-$20.

Plymouth Rock Gelatine Dainties, ca. 1910. 6 pages, 3.5" x 5.75". $10-$15.

They Know the Difference! Post Toasties, 1924. Postum Cereal Company. 2 page leaflet, 3" x 4.75". $5-$10.

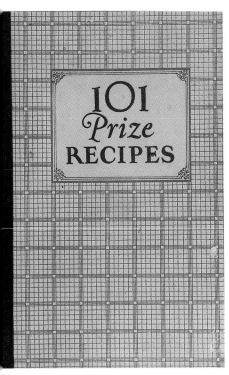

101 Prize Recipes, 1925. Postum Cereal Company, Inc. 40 pages, 4.25" x 6.25". $10-$15.

PRESTO CAKE FLOUR

Some Good Things to Bake, ca. 1920s. Hecker H-Q Company, Inc. 44 pages, 5" x 7". $10-$15.

101 Prize Recipes, 1928. Postum Cereal Company, Inc. 40 pages, 4" x 6.25". $5-$10.

PREMIER FOOD PRODUCTS

PURITAN FLOUR

The School Lunch, 1928. Postum Company, Inc. This was published as a guide for school lunch programs. 32 pages, 5.5" x 8". $10-$15.

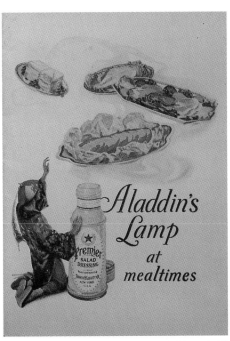

Aladdin's Lamp at Mealtimes, 1927. Francis H. Leggett & Company. 48 pages, 4.25" x 6". $10-$15.

How to Cook a Husband and Other Things, 1904. Wells-Abbott-Neiman Company. This book has a humorous introduction, "In selecting your husband do not go to market for him, as the best are brought to your door," and "They are apt to fall out of the kettle, and to be burned and crusty on the edges, since, like crabs and lobsters, you have to cook them while alive." 32 pages, 5" x 6.75". $30-$35.

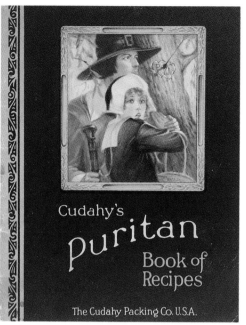

Cudahy's Puritan Book of Recipes, 1924. The Cudahy Packing Company. 28 pages, 5" x 6.25". $10-$15.

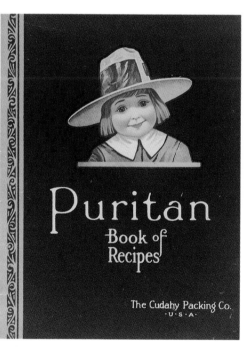

Puritan Book of Recipes, 1924. The Cudahy Packing Company. 28 pages, 5" x 6.5". $10-$15.

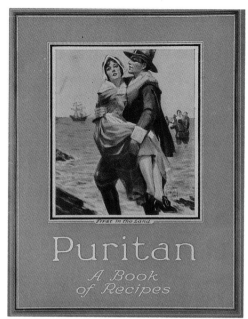

Puritan A Book of Recipes, ca. 1928. The Cudahy Packing Company. John Bradshaw Crandell (1896-1966) illustrated the front covers of these Puritan cookbooks. He also illustrated covers of *Cosmopolitan Magazine* for twelve years during the 1930s and 1940s. This edition included a coupon for 10 cents off the purchase of Puritan Bacon. 20 pages, 5" x 6.5". $10-$15.

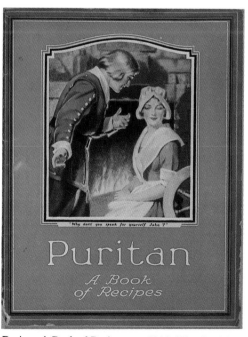

Puritan A Book of Recipes, ca. 1928. The Cudahy Packing Company. 26 pages, 5" x 6.5". $10-$15.

The Quaker brand of oatmeal was created by The Quaker Mill Company in Ravenna, Ohio in 1877. The company merged with The German Mills American Oatmeal Factory and together were renamed The Consolidated Oatmeal Company in 1886. Due to financial difficulties, Consolidated went out of business two years later. In 1888, the partners, Henry Parsons Crowell, Robert Stuart, and Ferdinand Schumacher, were instrumental in the merger of seven of the largest oatmeal millers in the United States. They named the business The American Cereal Company.

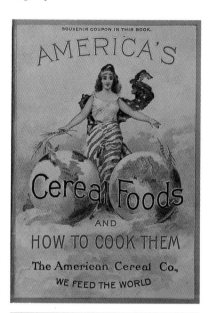

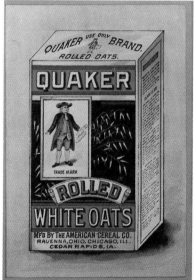

America's Cereal Foods and How to Cook Them, 1894 (shown front and back). This book contained a World's Fair Souvenir Coupon for a complete set of lithographs displayed at the Agriculture Building Exhibit. 68 pages, 4.5" x 6.75". $60-$70.

Crowell wanted to change the way oatmeal was purchased. Oatmeal had always been sold in bulk, resulting in many reports of unsanitary conditions. Incidents included grocers trimming their nails then mixing them in the barrels, cats napping on the oatmeal, and even rat traps set on top of open barrels. Around 1891, the product was introduced in distinctive four-color cardboard packages, conveying more of the symbol of purity. To help promote the newly packaged product the company filled entire trains with Quaker Oats. They hired five men to dress as Quakers who jumped down at each stop and gave free samples between Cedar Rapids, Iowa, and Portland, Oregon.

In 1897, a huge Quaker sign was posted on the famous White Cliffs in Dover, England. Incoming ships could see the sign as far as three miles away. This advertising stunt was very successful due to negative publicity. It actually took an act of parliament to get it removed.

In 1901, the American Cereal Company was renamed The Quaker Oats Company.

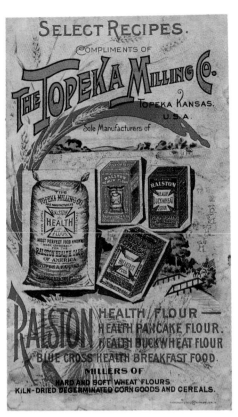

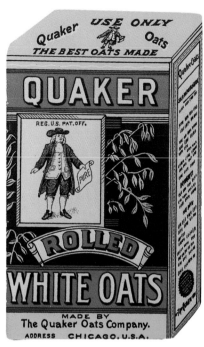

Quaker Rolled White Oats, ca. 1910s. The Quaker Oats Company. Attractive die-cut book. 12 pages, 3.25" x 5.25". $45-$50.

Select Recipes, ca. 1896. Ralston Health Flour, The Topeka Milling Company. This is one of the earlier products produced by The Robinson Danforth Company, which manufactured Purina cereal. In 1902, the company name was changed to The Ralston Purina Company. 16 pages, 3.75" x 6". $15-$20.

1920 Purina Book, 1920. Ralston Purina Company. 64 pages, 4" x 9". $10-$15.

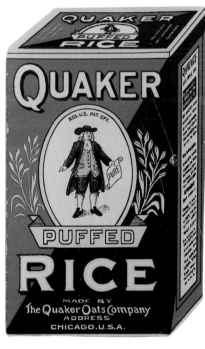

Quaker Puffed Rice, ca. 1910s. The Quaker Oats Company. Attractive die-cut book. 8 pages, 3.25" x 5.25". $45-$50.

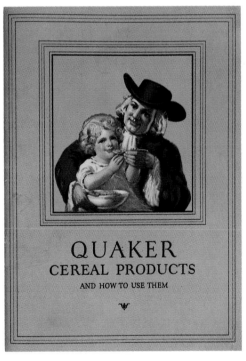

Quaker Cereal Products and How to Use Them, 1927. 56 pages, 5" x 7". $25-$30.

RELIABLE FLOUR

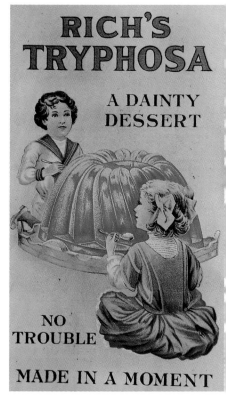

A Mother's Manual, 1928. Ralston Purina Company. 32 pages, 4.25" x 6.25". $10-$15.

Would you like to make Good Cake? ca. 1910s. Reliable Flour Company. 2 page leaflet, 3.25" x 6.25". $5-$10.

Rich's Tryphosa A Dainty Dessert, ca. 1890s. E. C. Rich. Beautiful illustrations. 8 pages, 3.5" x 6". $25-$30.

RED STAR FLOUR

RIPPEY'S EXTRACTS

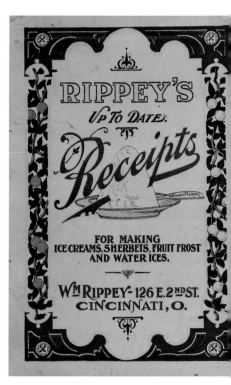

Red Star Flour, ca. 1925. The Red Star Milling Company. 6 pages, with 4 page fold out, 3.5" x 6.25". $5-$10.

Delicious Strawberry Shortcake, ca. 1920s. Reliable Flour Company. 2 page fold out, 3.25" x 6.25". $5-$10.

Rippey's Up To Date Receipts, ca. 1890s. W. M. Rippey. 16 pages, 4.75" x 7". $20-$25.
A Mother's Manual, 1928. Ralston Purina Company. 32 pages, 4.25" x 6.25". $10-$15.

ROYAL BAKING POWDER

A small drug store located in Fort Wayne, Indiana was the birthplace of the Royal Baking Powder Company in 1865. Two druggists, Thomas M. Biddle and J.C. Hoagland, were trying to invent a new formula for leavening flour. The usual method required the addition of baking powder and an acid such as sour milk or vinegar to activate the soda. The druggists discovered that by equally combining cream of tarter and baking soda they could produce a better product with satisfactory results. Housewives and bakers welcomed the new product, for it meant a faster and safer process of baking.

The partners moved manufacturing operations to Chicago in 1875, then on to New York City, where the merger of Standard Brands was created in 1929.

Royal Baker and Pastry Cook, 1896. 44 pages, 5" x 8". $30-$35.

Royal Baker and Pastry Cook, 1906. 44 pages, 5" x 8". $20-$25.

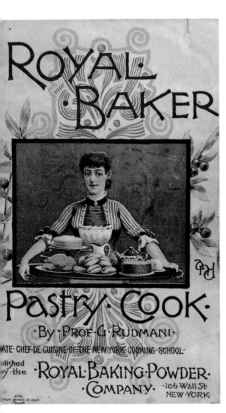

Royal Baker Pastry Cook, 1888. 42 pages, 5" x 8.25". $30-$35.

Royal Baker and Pastry Cook, 1902. 44 pages, 5.25" x 8". $20-$25.

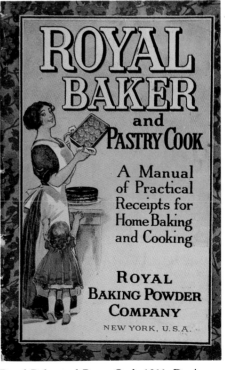

Royal Baker and Pastry Cook, 1911. During World War I, stickers were placed on the front giving instructions on conserving eggs. 44 pages, 5" x 7.75". $20-$25.

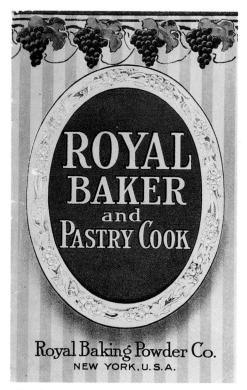

Royal Baker and Pastry Cook, 1913. 46 pages, 5" x 8". $15-$20.

New Royal Cook Book, 1922. 50 pages, 5" x 8". $5-$10.

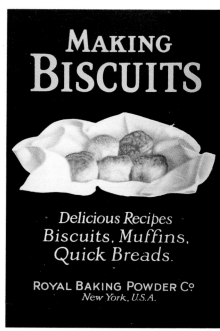

Making Biscuits, 1927. 14 pages, 5" x 7". $5-$10.

55 Ways to Save Eggs, 1917. 22 pages, 4.5" x 6.75". $10-$15.

Royal Baking Powder, ca. 1925. Chinese edition cookbook, back of book stamped "Sales Corporation, Shanghai." 42 pages, 6" x 7.25". $20-$25.

Royal Cook Book, 1929. 49 pages, 5.25" x 8". $5-$10.

Something Better! Royal Gelatine Desserts, 1925. Royal Baking Powder Company. 3 page fold out, 4" x 6.25". $5-$10.

ROYAL SALAD DRESSING

How to Make Salads, ca. 1894. Royal Salad Dressing, Horton-Cato Manufacturing Company. 16 pages, 4.5" x 5.5". $25-$30.

Royal Yeast Bake Book, ca. 1915. E. W. Gillette Company, Ltd. 32 pages, 3.5" x 6". $10-$15.

RUMFORD BAKING POWDER
(Also see Horsford's)

George F. Wilson joined a partnership with Professor E. N. Horsford of Harvard University. By 1857, their business was incorporated under the name Rumford Chemical Works. During that time France was the main producer of cream of tarter and the prices were high. One of the first

Royal Fruit Gelatin Suggestions, 1926 (shown front and back). Royal Baking Powder Company. 16 pages, 6" x 7.25". $10-$15.

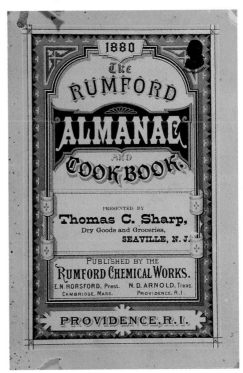

The Rumford Almanac and Cookbook, 1880. Rumford Chemical Works. 48 pages, 4.75" x 7". $50-$60. Courtesy of Nick and Nancy DeShetler.

chemicals to be introduced by the company was acid calcium phosphate, a more affordable substitute. The next year they introduced Rumford Yeast Powder, a combination of calcium phosphate and bicarbonate soda. This product would not only raise dough, it restored all the healthful elements that were lost during the process of milling white flour. As a result, Rumford was the first to truly introduce baking powder to the world.

Rumford Chemical Works was originally located in Seekonk, Massachusetts. The partners were satisfied with the company name, but Wilson wasn't happy with the name of the area. The processing factory was located next to the river which separated Rhode Island and Massachusetts. Rather than move the factory, Wilson set out to move Rhode Island. It took around a decade to do it, but he succeeded. A portion of Pawtucket was traded by the Rhode Island Legislature for that portion of Massachusetts which is now called Rumford, Rhode Island.

The Horsford/Rumford almanacs and cookbooks are considered highly collectible due to their attractive covers and illustrations of small children.

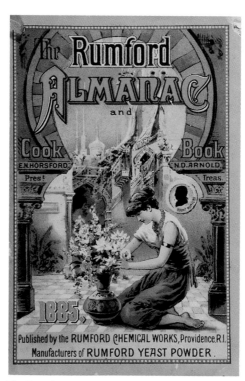

The Rumford Almanac and Cookbook, 1885. Rumford Chemical Works. 36 pages, 4.75" x 7". $50-$55. *Courtesy of Nick and Nancy DeShetler.*

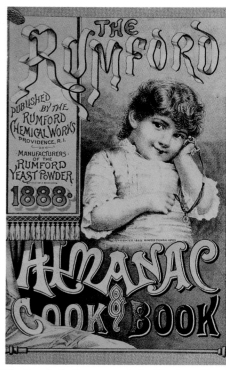

The Rumford Almanac and Cookbook, 1888. Rumford Chemical Works. 36 pages, 4.75" x 7". $40-$45. *Courtesy of Nick and Nancy DeShetler.*

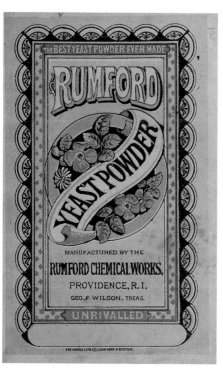

Rumford Yeast Powder, ca. 1880s. Rumford Chemical Works. 2 page leaflet, 3.25" x 5". $20-$25. *Courtesy of Nick and Nancy DeShetler.*

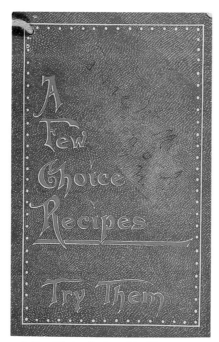

A Few Choice Recipes, Try Them, ca. 1887. Rumford Chemical Works. 12 pages, 3.25" x 5". $20-$25. *Courtesy of Nick and Nancy DeShetler.*

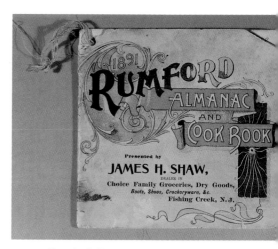

Rumford Almanac and Cook Book, 1891. Rumford Chemical Works. 36 pages, 4.75" x 4.75". $40-$45. *Courtesy of Nick and Nancy DeShetler.*

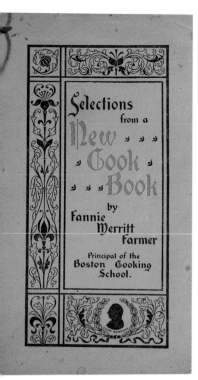

Selections from a New Cook Book, 1896. Written by Fannie Merritt Farmer, Rumford Chemical Works. 1896 pages, 3.5" x 6". $25-$35. *Courtesy of Nick and Nancy DeShetler.*

Rumford Cook Book, 1898. Rumford Chemical Works. 48 pages, 4.25" x 6.5". $40-$45.

Rumford Cook Book, 1903. Rumford Chemical Works. 48 pages, 3.75" x 7.5". $40-$45. *Courtesy of Nick and Nancy DeShetler.*

Cake, ca. 1898. Rumford Chemical Works, side clasp. 16 pages, 3.5" x 6". $20-$25. *Courtesy of Nick and Nancy DeShetler.*

Ten Tempting Receipts, 1901. Rumford Chemical Works. 8 pages, 3.5" x 6.25". $40-$45. *Courtesy of Nick and Nancy DeShetler.*

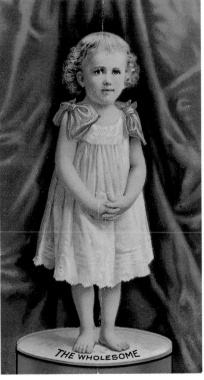

Rumford Cook Book, 1903. Rumford Chemical Works. 8 pages, 3.5" x 6.25". $40-$45. *Courtesy of Nick and Nancy DeShetler.*

Rumford, 1904. Rumford Chemical Works, rare. 8 pages, 3.5" x 6.5". $40-$45.

Rumford Receipt Book, 1906. Rumford Chemical Works. 20 pages, 6" x 9.25". $45-$50.

Rumford, The Wholesome Baking Powder, 1907. Rumford Chemical Works. 8 pages, 3.5" x 6.5". $35-$40. *Courtesy of Nick and Nancy DeShetler.*

Compliments of Rumford, 1905. Rumford Chemical Works. 8 pages, 3.5" x 6.25". $35-$45.

California Receipts, 1907. Rumford Chemical Works. 36 pages, 3.75" x 6". $20-$25. *Courtesy of Nick and Nancy DeShetler.*

Rumford Cook Book, 1908. Rumford Chemical Works. 48 pages, 4.5" x 7". $20-$25.

Compliments of Rumford, 1908. Rumford Chemical Works. 12 pages, 3.25" x 6.5". 35-$40.

Rumford Receipt Book, 1909. Rumford Chemical Works. 20 pages, 6" x 9.25". $45-$50.

Rumford Receipt Book, 1909. Rumford Chemical Works. 20 pages, 6" x 9.25". $45-$50.

Rumford Receipt Book, 1908. 20 pages, 6" x 9.25". $45-$50. *Courtesy of James Welsh, Jr.*

Compliments of Rumford, 1909. Rumford Chemical Works. 14 pages, 3.5" x 6.25". $35-$40.

Untitled, Rumford Cook Book, 1909. Rumford Chemical Works. 12 pages, 3.5" x 6.25". $25-$30.

Rumford Receipt Book, 1911. Rumford Chemical Works. 24 pages, 6" x 9.25". $45-$50.

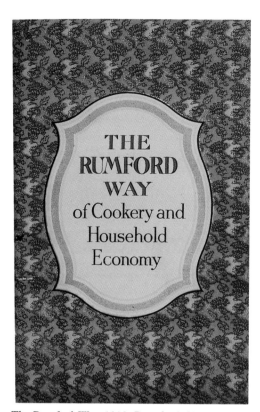

THE RUMFORD WAY of Cookery and Household Economy

The Rumford Way, 1912. Rumford Chemical Works. 68 pages, 4.5" x 7.25". $20-$30.

Untitled, Rumford Cook Book, 1913. Rumford Chemical Works. 32 pages, 3.5" x 6.25". $25-$30.

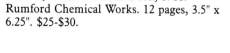

Untitled, Rumford Cook Book, 1911. Rumford Chemical Works. 12 pages, 3.5" x 6.25". $25-$30.

Rumford Recipe Book, 1913. Rumford Chemical Works. 24 pages, 6" x 9.25". $45-$50.

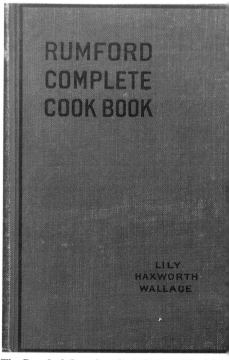

RUMFORD COMPLETE COOK BOOK

LILY HAXWORTH WALLACE

The Rumford Complete Cook Book, 1918. Lily Haxworth Wallace, Rumford Chemical Works, hard cover. 240 pages, 5" x 7.25". $15-$20.

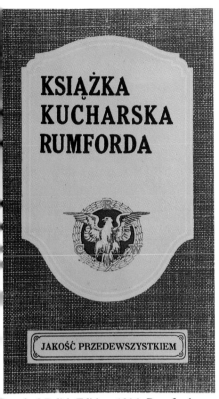

Rumford Polish Edition, 1916. Rumford Chemical Works. 24 pages, 3.75" x 6.25". $20-$25. *Courtesy of Nick and Nancy DeShetler.*

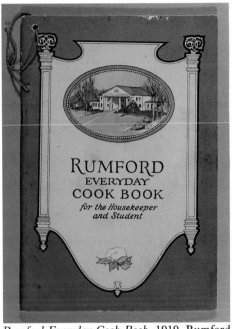

Rumford Everyday Cook Book, 1919. Rumford Chemical Works. 64 pages, 5" x 7". $20-$25.

Playing Cook, A Selection of Choice Recipes, ca. 1920. Rumford Chemical Works. 2 page folder, 3.5" x 6.25". $10-$15.

Rumford Dainties, 1919. Rumford Chemical Works. 8 pages, 2.25" x 3.75". $15-$20. *Courtesy of Nick and Nancy DeShetler.*

How's That Grandma? A Selection of Choice Recipes, 1920. Rumford Chemical Works. 2 page folder, 3.5" x 6.25". $10-$15.

Rumford Fruit Cook Book, 1927. Rumford Chemical Works. 48 pages, 4.75" x 6.75". $20-$30.

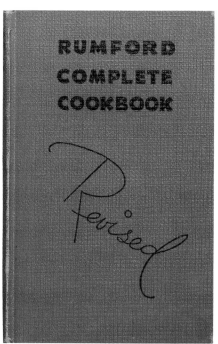

The Rumford Complete Cook Book Revised, 1940. Lily Haxworth Wallace, Rumford Company, hard cover. 209 pages, 5" x 7.25". $10-$15.

RYZON BAKING POWDER

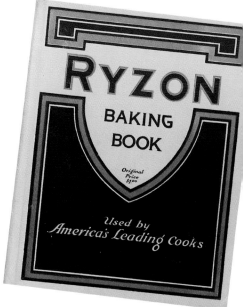

Giving Delicacy and Flavor To Daily Cooking by the New Use of Rumford, 1932. Rumford Chemical Works. 32 pages, 4.75" x 6.5". $15-$25.

RUNKEL CHOCOLATE

Ryzon Baking Book - Used by America's Leading Cooks, 1918. Marion Harris Neil, General Chemical Company, hard cover. 74 pages, 6.5" x 8". $15-$20.

Runkel's New Cocoa Cookery, ca. 1920s. Runkel Brothers, Inc. 36 pages, 4.5" x 6". $10-$15.

Chapter 7 Food Brands: Sauer's to Yeast Foam

AUER'S

0 Recipes for Flavoring by a Famous Chef, ca.
900s. The C. F. Sauer Company. 21 pages,
.5" x 6". $5-$10.

Choice Flavoring Recipes, ca. 1920s. The C. F.
auer Company. 24 pages, 3.5" x 6". $10-$15.

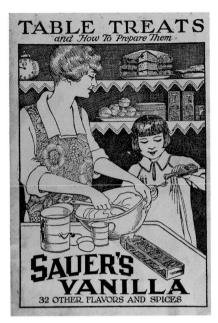

Table Treats and How to Prepare Them, ca.
1920s. The C. F. Sauer Company. 30 pages,
5.75" x 8.5". $10-$15.

*Table Treats, Good Things to Eat And How to
Prepare Them*, ca. 1923. The C. F. Sauer
Company. 30 pages, 5.75" x 8.5". $10-$15.

SAVOY FOODS

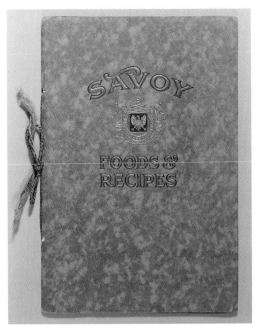

Savoy Foods and Recipes, ca. 1920s. Steele-
Wedeles Company. 30 pages, 5.5" x 8".
$10-$15.

SHREDDED WHEAT CEREAL

A delicate stomach and chronic indiges-
tion is what prompted Henry Perky, a Nebraska lawyer, to invent a highly digestible
cereal called "Shredded Wheat." Experimenting, he found that boiled whole wheat
was soft and absorbent. He invented a machine that would press the wheat into

The Vital Question, ca. 1897. The Cereal
Machine Company, cloth cover. 146 pages, 4"
x 4.5". $40-$45.

shred-like strips, so the customer could create their own product at home. He formed the Cereal Machine Company with his brother John in 1892, but their success was short lived. The consumer was simply not interested.

Perky was determined to try again and one year later he invented a baked, not boiled, shredded-strip biscuit that was easy to distribute. He opened a bakery where he created delicious dishes and sold the cereal door to door. When sales were prosperous, he established factories in Boston and Massachusetts. By the 1900s, the Natural Food Company had become successor to The Shredded Wheat Company and Perky had moved his business to Niagara Falls, New York. He opened the "Palace of Light" factory which became known as the "World's Finest Food Factory." It was decked out in marble, tile, and glass. They welcomed millions of visitors who toured the factory in air-conditioned comfort. The National Biscuit Company acquired the Shredded Wheat Company in 1928. The original formula, with the absence of sugars, salt, and artificial flavors, remains one of the most popular health food cereals produced today.

More Light, ca. 1898. The Natural Food Company. 18 pages, 3" x 5". $25-$30.

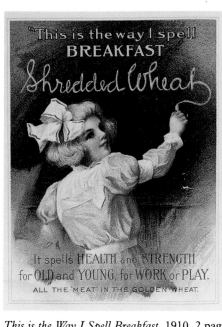

This is the Way I Spell Breakfast, 1910. 2 page leaflet, 4.75" x 6". $15-$20.

More Light, ca. 1898. The Cereal Machine Company. 18 pages, 3" x 5". $25-$30.

Souvenir Menu, 1906. This was a souvenir at the Banquet to the National Association of Retail Grocers hosted by The Natural Food Company. No recipes. 4 pages, 5.25" x 9". $10-$15.

Crisp and Tasty! Triscuit, ca. 1920s. 2 page leaflet, 3.75" x 5.75". $10-$15.

For All Ages Shredded Wheat, ca. 1920s. 14 pages, 4.75" x 5.75". $10-$15.

"What do you eat? I eat Shredded Wheat," ca. 1920s. The Shredded Wheat Company. 6 pages, 4.5" x 6". $10-$15.

Recipes for New and Delicious Energy Dishes, 1933. 17 pages, 4" x 7". $15-$20.

SINCLAIR'S MEATS

Health from the Whole Wheat, ca. 1920s. 68 pages, 5" x 6.75". $25-$30.

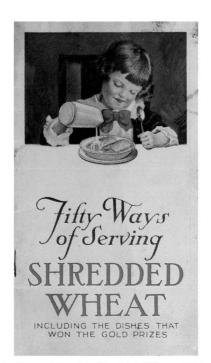

Fifty Ways of Serving Shredded Wheat, 1924. 20 pages, 3.5" x 6". $15-$20.

Sinclair's Fidelity Meats, 1902. T. M. Sinclair & Company Ltd. 6 pages, 3.5" x 6". $20-$25.

Sinclair's Fidelity Meats, 1902. T. M. Sinclair & Company Ltd. 6 pages, 3.5" x 6". $20-$25.

SLADES
(Also see Congress Baking Powder)

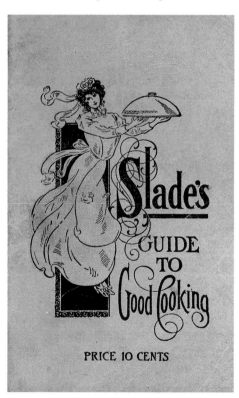

Slade's Guide to Good Cooking, 1907. 66 pages, 4.5" x 7". $20-$25.

SLEEPY EYE FLOUR

Sleepy Eye Flour was named after an Indian chief called Old Sleepy Eye of the Lower Sissenton Sioux tribe. In 1824, the tribe sent him to Washington D. C. to receive the honorary title "Chief" from President Monroe because of his devoted friendship to the white man. After the Chicago and Northwestern Railroad was established in 1872, Sleepy Eye, Minnesota became a town. The Sleepy Eye Milling Company was established in 1883, and quality flour was shipped to all parts of the country. The popular Indian trademark became a huge success in 1904 at the St. Louis World's Fair, where Sleepy Eye Flour was awarded the Grand Prize.

Sleepy Eye Cook Book, ca. 1904. Sleepy Eye Milling Company. Die-cut book, extremely rare. 96 pages, 5" x 4.5". $150-$165.

SNOWDRIFT SHORTENING

Snowdrift Secrets, 1912. The Southern Cotton Oil Company. Wonderful artwork, highly collectible among Black Memorabilia collectors. 48 pages, 5" x 7". $50-$70.

Snowdrift, ca. 1925. Advertising die-cut. 3 page fold out, 4" x 5.25" unfolded, 8" x 9.5". $10-$15.

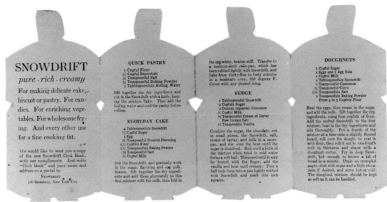

Snowdrift, ca. 1920s. Advertising die-cut. Popular among Black Memorabilia collectors. 4 page fold out, 3" x 6". $20-$25.

SNOW KING BAKING POWDER

Tempting Pastries, ca. 1920. The Willis Norton Company, nice illustrations. 4 pages, 3.5" x 6". $10-$15.

Better Baking Recipes, ca. 1920. 21 pages, 5.75" x 3.5". $15-$20.

SOUTHERN RICE GROWERS ASSOCIATION

American Grown Rice, The Ideal Food, ca. 1911. Southern Rice Growers Association. 24 pages, 3.5" x 6.25". $5-$10.

Famous Baking Recipes, 1929. Nice illustrations! 28 pages, 6" x 3". $10-$15.

Aunt Jenny's Favorite Recipes, ca. 1940s. Lever Brothers Company. 49 pages, 6" x 7.25". $5-$10.

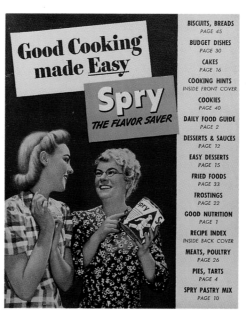

Good Cooking Made Easy, 1942. Lever Brothers Company. 48 pages, 6" x 7.25". $5-$10.

Home Baking Made Easy for Beginners and Experts, 1953. Lever Brothers Company. 23 pages, 5.25" x 7.5". $5-$10.

What Shall I Cook Today? ca. 1940s. Lever Brothers Company. 48 pages, 6" x 7.25". $5-$10.

12 Pies Husbands Like Best, ca. 1950s. Lever Brothers Company. 21 pages, 5.25" x 7.5". $5-$10.

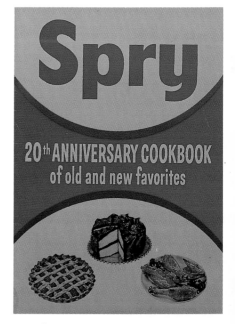

Spry 20th Anniversary Cookbook, 1955. Lever Brothers Company. This book was produced to celebrate the 20th anniversary of Spry, even though the product was discontinued shortly thereafter due to stiff competition with Crisco. 25 pages, 5.25" x 7.5". $5-$10.

STALEY'S SYRUP

The A. E. Staley Company was established by Augustus Eugene Staley in 1906. Staley bought corn starch in bulk bags, repackaged it in one pound boxes, and named as his own product, Cream Corn Starch. A factory soon opened in Decatur, Illinois and he manufactured corn starch as well as becoming the second largest corn processor in the United States.

Staley's Approved Recipes, 1928. A. E. Staley Mfg. Company. 30 pages, 4.75" x 6.5". $10-$15.

Staley's Approved Recipes, 1924. A. E. Staley Mfg. Company. 23 pages, 3.5" x 6.25". $10-$15.

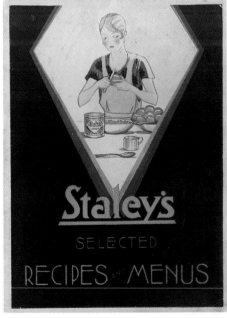

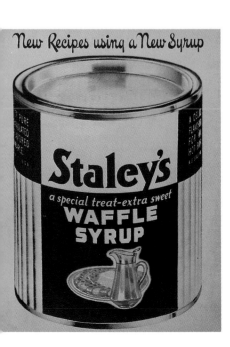

Above:
Staley's Selected Recipes Menus, ca. 1930s. A. E. Staley Mfg. Company. 64 pages, 4.75" x 6.5". $10-$15.

Left:
New Recipes Using a New Syrup, ca. 1920s. A. E. Staley Mfg. Company. 2 page leaflet, 5" x 6.25". $5-$10.

Right:
Busy-Day Salads and Desserts, ca. 1920s. California Fruit Growers Exchange. 16 pages, 4.75" x 6.5". $10-$15.

SUNKIST ORANGES

The Sunkist brand name was adopted in 1908 by the Southern California Fruit Exchange, which was a cooperative of California Citrus Fruit Growers. The term "Sunkissed" was coined by an advertising agency copywriter. They continued to use this name in newspaper advertisements until later it was shortened to just "Sunkist."

In an effort to help consumers find other uses for citrus fruit, a new product was introduced in 1916. This newly designed and advertised glass hand-reamer allowed consumers to squeeze their own fresh citrus juice. Thus, the "Drink an Orange" slogan was adopted.

Originally, the Sunkist trademark was stamped on tissue paper that covered each piece of fruit. In 1925, the trademark was stamped on the fruit itself.

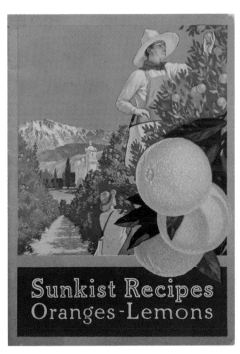

Sunkist Recipes Oranges-Lemons, 1916. California Fruit Growers Exchange. 64 pages, 4.75" x 6.75". $10-$15.

Sunkist New-Day Drinks, 1922. California Fruit Growers Exchange. 16 pages, 4.75" x 6.75". $10-$15.

SUN MAID RAISINS

Sun Maid Raisins, 1921. California Associated Raisin Company. 26 pages, 3.75" x 6.5". $20-$25.

New Interest in Simple Menus with Famous Sun-Maid Recipes, 1926. Sun-Maid Growers Association. 48 pages, 4.75" x 6.75". $5-$10.

For Vigorous Health - Sunkist Recipes for Every Day, 1936. California Fruit Growers Exchange. 48 pages, 5" x 7.5". $5-$10.

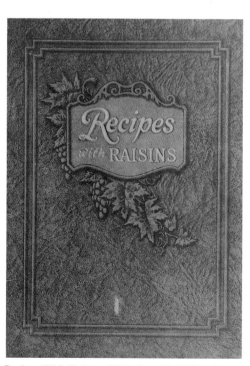

Recipes With Raisins, 1923. Sun-Maid Raisin Growers Association. 46 pages, 5" x 6.75". $10-$15.

Famous Cooks' Recipes for Raisin Cookery, 1926. Sun-Maid Raisin Growers Association of California. 32 pages, 5.5" x 7.75". $5-$10.

SWAN'S DOWN FLOUR

Farmer Levi Igleheart, discouraged with his profession at the age of thirty-three, decided to start a saw mill in the little town of Evansville bordering the Ohio River and Erie Canal in 1853. He also began grinding corn and wheat. The new enterprise was so prosperous that his two brothers, Asa and William, soon joined him. They named the firm Igleheart Brothers, Millers. Asa later resigned to pursue the legal profession. The company incorporated by 1892, and shortly after William died. Levi and his three sons, Leslie, Addison, and John, continued to run the business, successfully developing the superior grade of Swan's Down Cake Flour.

Swan's Down Cake Flour Recipes, ca. 1915. Igleheart Brothers. 10 pages, 3" x 4.5". $10-$15.

Cake Secrets, 1915. Igleheart Brothers. 36 pages, 4.25" x 5.75". $10-$15.

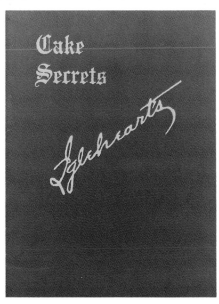

Cake Secrets, 1922. Igleheart Brothers. 32 pages, 4.75" x 7". $10-$15.

Cake Secrets, 1928. Postum Company Incorporated. 36 pages, 4.5" x 7". $10-$15.

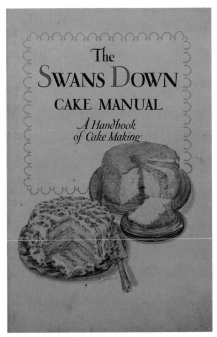

The Swan's Down Cake Manual, 1929. Postum Company Incorporated. 48 pages, 5.75" x 8.75". $10-$15.

SWIFT'S MEAT

Gustavus Franklin Swift was sixteen years old when he started his career in the meat packing business. While working for his brother, the town butcher, and moonlighting at night, he managed to buy a steer once a week. He then butchered the meat and sold it to local housewives door to door.

Swift's Cotosuet, ca. 1906. Swift & Company. Attractive die-cut book. 12 pages, 3.5" x 5". $35-$40.

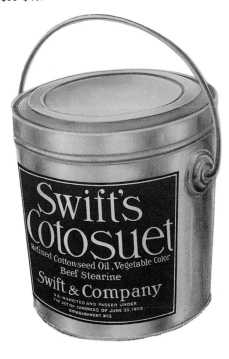

Four years later he opened his own butcher shop. He continued to prosper, opening distributing centers in nearby communities and using meat wagons to provide the daily routes. His success attracted the attention of James A. Hathaway, a large commercial Boston meat packer, which eventually led to the partnership of Hathaway & Swift.

Swift was creative in the use of meat by-products, developing them into oleo margarine, glue, soaps, and fertilizer. His real knowledge and insight were demonstrated in 1877, when he sent the first Chicago-dressed beef to Boston by a special railroad car designed to prevent the spoilage of meat by the use of blocks of ice, thus cutting the high cost of transporting live animals. Swift later invented his own version of the refrigerated car, and developed a more efficient, economical system of meat packing.

Swift dissolved his partnership with Hathaway and formed Swift Bros. & Company with his brother Edwin in 1878. After his death in 1903, his four sons gained control and management of the company, continuing to make it as successful as it is today.

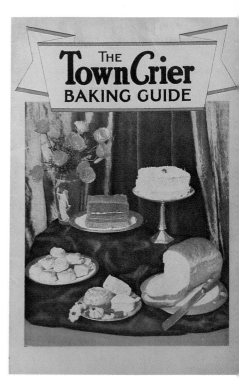

TOWN CRIER FLOUR

The Town Crier Baking Guide, ca. 1930's. The Midland Flour Milling Company. 24 pages, 5" x 7.5". $10-$15.

The Kitchen Encyclopedia, 1911. Swift & Company. 30 pages, 5" x 8.5". $15-$20.

Town Crier Ready Mixed Flour Recipes, ca. 1920s. Town Crier Food Products, Inc. Attractive die-cut book. 16 pages, 4" x 5.5". $25-$30.

UNITED FRUIT

The Story of the Banana, 1927. United Fruit Company. 24 pages, 6" x 9". $10-$15.

Town Crier Ready Mixed Flour Recipes, ca. 1920s. Town Crier Food Products, Inc. This small booklet was also available in many languages. 16 pages, 2" x 4.25". $15-$20.

ICTOR COFFEE

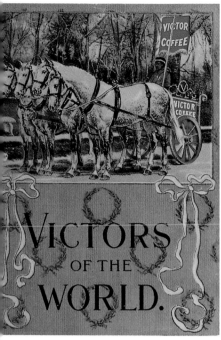

Victors of the World, 1898. Shapleigh Coffee Company. 16 pages, 4.25" x 5.75". $15-$20.

ALKER'S CHILE

Walker's Red Hot Chile Con Carne, 1918. Walker Properties Association. 16 pages, 3" x 75". $10-$15.

WEDGWOOD BUTTER

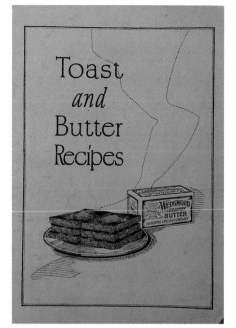

Toast and Butter Recipes, 1924. Harding Cream Company. 8 pages, 5.25" x 7.5". $5-$10.

WELCH'S GRAPE JUICE

Thomas Welch, a dedicated Prohibitionist and a devoted religious man, was determined to formulate a non-alcoholic grape beverage that his Methodist church could use during Communion. Living in Vineland, New Jersey, grapes were plentiful and he began experimenting in the family kitchen every evening. He soon discovered that by boiling the bottled filtered grape juice, the yeast microorganisms were killed, thus preventing the natural fermentation process.

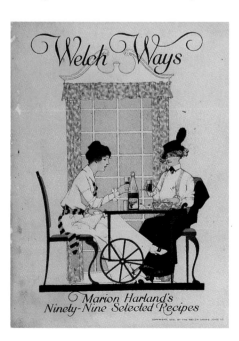

In 1869, the first bottles of Dr. Welch's Unfermented Wine were ready, but the church frowned on using nothing but the real thing for Communion. His plans were abandoned until his son, Charles Welch, believed he had a solution for selling his father's grape juice—through advertising.

Charles recognized the need for public appeal, and utilizing popular temperance themes of the 1890s, he changed the name of the juice to Dr. Welch's Grape Juice. In 1893, he renamed the beverage to its current name of Welch's Grape Juice. He exhibited the product at the Chicago World's Fair in 1893, the Atlantic Boardwalk, conventions, and numerous fairs. But the most important promotion for the juice came with the passing of the Fifteenth Amendment in 1919, prohibiting the making or drinking of alcoholic beverages. The popularity of Welch's Grape Juice soared and it is still a favorite drink enjoyed by Americans today.

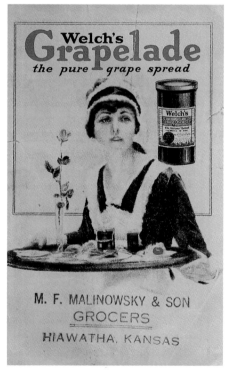

Welch's Grapelade, 1923. The Welch Grape Juice Company added the word "jelly" in 1923. Inside: "...Grapelade was first made and packed for our armies in France to give them 'A Sweet Taste of Home.'" 2 page leaflet, 3.5" x 5.5". $5-$10.

Welch Ways, 1915. The Welch Grape Juice Company, nice illustrations. 28 pages, 4.75" x 6.25". $15-$20.

WESSON OIL

Recipe Book, 1910. The Southern Cotton Oil Company. 13 pages, 3" x 4". $5-$10.

Home Made Salad Dressings, ca. 1920s. Wesson Oil, attractive die-cut. 4 page fold out, 3.25" x 6". $15-$20.

Recipes, 1911. The Southern Oil Company. 56 pages, 5" x 7". $15-$20.

Salads-With Wesson Oil, 1926. Wesson Oil & Snowdrift People. 35 pages, 4.25" x 6". $5-$10.

Wheatlet Breakfast Food, 1895. The Franklin Mills Company. This is actually two books combined in one. The reverse is a Franklin Mills Fine Flour cookbook. 24 pages, 3.25" x 5.5". $25-$30.

WHITE CREST FLOUR

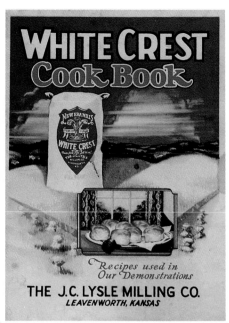

White Crest Cook Book, ca. 1915. The J. C. Lysle Milling Company. 12 pages, 4.5" x 6". $10-$15.

WILBUR'S COCOA

Wilbur's Cocoa, 1912. Attractive die-cut booklet. H.O. Wilbur & Sons. 8 pages, 3.75" x 4.5". $60-$70.

Cook's Tours Through Wilburland, 1912. 40 pages, 3.25" x 6". $25-$30.

WHITMAN'S CHOCOLATE

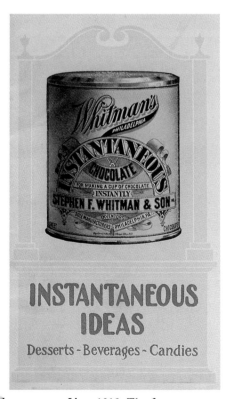

Instantaneous Ideas, 1912. The famous Whitman's Sampler Chocolate Box first appeared in 1912. This cookbook by Stephen Whitman showed his talent by introducing recipes such as Chocolate Mint Creams, Chocolate Sea Foam with Nuts, and Chocolate Cocoanut Nougat. 24 pages, 3.5" x 6". $15-$20.

WILKEN WHISKEY

The Wilken Family Home Cooking Album, 1935. Finch & Company. 48 pages, 9.5" x 5.5". $10-$15.

The Wilken Family Home Entertaining Album, 1937. The Wilken Family, Inc. 40 pages, 9.5" x 5.5". $10-$15.

WILSON'S MEAT

WONDER BREAD

WRIGHT'S SMOKE

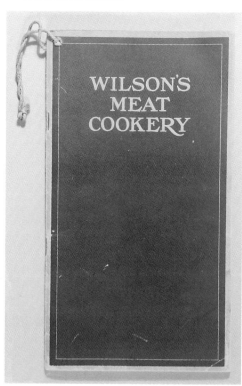

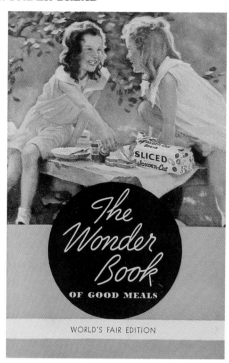

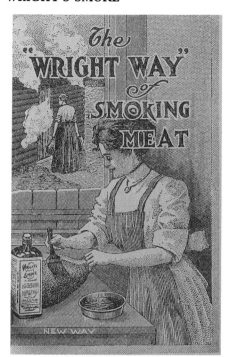

Wilson's Meat Cookery, 1919. Wilson & Company. 64 pages, 5.25" x 9.25". $15-$20.

The Wonder Book of Good Meals, 1934. Continental Baking Company. This book was given away as a souvenir from the Wonder Bakery Exhibit at the Chicago's World's Fair in 1933. 32 pages, 4.75" x 7.5". $10-$15.

The "Wright Way" of Smoking Meat, 1910. The E. H. Wright Company, Ltd. 32 pages, 3.25" x 5". $20-$25.

WILSON'S MILK

WOODCOCK MACARONI

Wilson's New Recipes, ca. 1920s. Indiana Condensed Milk Company. 18 pages, 5.25" x 6.5". $10-$15.

Fifty Good Ways of Serving Woodcock Macaroni, 1919. John G. Elbs. 16 pages, 4.25" x 6". $10-$15.

Cured with Wright's Ham Pickle and Smoked with Wright's Smoke, ca. 1920s. The E. H. Wright Company, Ltd. 32 pages, 5.25" x 7.75". $15-$20.

YEAST FOAM/MAGIC YEAST/MACA YEAST

The Northwestern Yeast Company was established during the 1880s in Chicago, Illinois. Yeast Foam and Magic Yeast were identical products sold under different names across the United States. Magic Yeast was patented in 1885. The company even had its own radio program called "The Yeast Foamers" which provided endorsements. Products also included Maca Yeast, Yeast Foam Tablets, and Animal Poultry Yeast Foam. Yeast was popular for beverages such as root beer and ginger ale, as well as for a health aid. Advertisements claimed that eating three yeast cakes a day could cure constipation, boils, acne, and rheumatism.

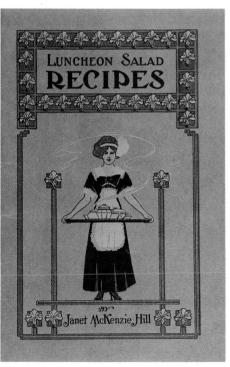

Yacht Club Manual of Salads, 1914. Tildesley & Company. 30 pages, 5" x 7.25". $10-$15.

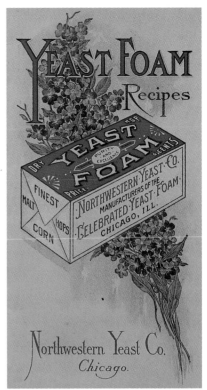

Yeast Foam Recipes, ca. 1890s. 8 pages, 3.25" x 6". $20-$25.

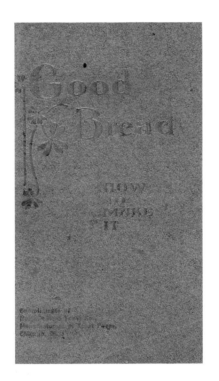

Good Bread How to Make It, 1890. 28 pages, 3.5" x 6". $20-$25.

Bake at Home Use Magic Yeast and Save Money, ca. 1900. 3 page fold out, 3.25" x 5.5". $10-$15.

Luncheon Salad Recipes, 1912. Written by Janet McKenzie Hill, Reid, Murdoch & Company. 32 pages, 5" x 7.25". $15-$20.

Bake at Home Use Magic Yeast, ca. 1910. 18 pages, 3" x 6". $10-$15.

Yeast Foam Recipes, ca. 1910. 12 pages, 6" x 3.25". $15-$20.

Magic Yeast Recipes, ca. 1910. 14 pages, 3" x 6". $15-$20.

Yeast Foam Recipes, ca. 1910. 12 pages, 3.25" x 6". $15-$20.

Yeast Foam Recipes, ca. 1915. 12 pages, 3.25" x 6". $15-$20.

Yeast Foam Recipes, ca. 1915. 12 pages, 3.25" x 6". $15-$20.

Yeast Foam Recipes, ca. 1915. 12 pages, 3.25" x ". $15-$20.

Dry Yeast as an Aid to Health, 1921. Advertising booklet, no recipes. Claims to cure boils, intestinal pains, headaches, constipation, and improve complexions. 12 pages, 3.75" x 6". $10-$15.

The Art of Making Bread, ca. 1920s. 20 pages with a 4 page fold out, 5" x 8". $12-$15.

Yeast Foam Recipes, ca. 1915. 12 pages, 3.25" x 5". $10-$15.

The Art of Making Bread, ca. 1920s. 20 pages, 5" x 8". $10-$15.

The Art of Making Bread…At Home, 1939. Maca Yeast, Northwestern Yeast Company. This book featured the famous "World of Tomorrow" pictured from the 1939 World's Fair in New York City. 20 pages, 4.75" x 7.5". $20-$25.

Chapter 8 Wartime Era

WORLD WAR I

During the years 1914-1918, Americans heard the slogan "Food will win the War!" To crush the Kaiser's dream of world domination many allied countries near starvation held the front lines until American troops could arrive. Hoover responded with an appeal to the American people to save wheat, meat, sugar, and fats to ship more of our food to our allies and our military. During the Conservation Days, the housewife's role was recognized for her sacrifice, creativity, and cooperation in the kitchen. Women developed new and imaginative ways of using below-grade war flour and wheat substitutes in their recipes. They used syrup instead of sugar as well as substitutes for lard, butter, and meat to feed their families. Cookbooks were published on this theme, and their recipes reflected the loyalty of the country.

How to Save Eggs by using Dr. Price's Cream Baking Powder, 1917. 22 pages, 4.5" x 6.75". $10-$15.

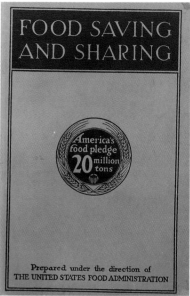

Food Saving and Sharing - America's Food Pledge 20 Million Tons, 1918. The United States Food Administration, Doubleday, Page & Company. Hard cover, 102 pages, 5.25" x 7.75". $15-$20.

The McNess Cook Book, ca. 1918. Furst-McNess Company. Has picture of soldier on back cover and discusses the end of the war, containing quotes such as "America must feed the world" and "Food saves lives don't waste it." 32 pages, 5.75" x 8.5". $15-$20.

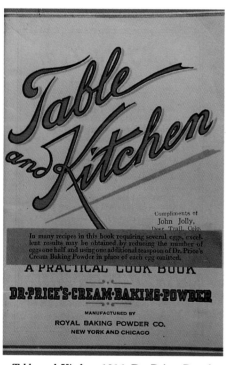

Table and Kitchen, 1916. Dr. Price, Royal Baking Powder. During World War I, blue stickers were placed on the covers giving instructions for baking with less eggs. 60 pages, 4.75" x 7.25". $15-$20.

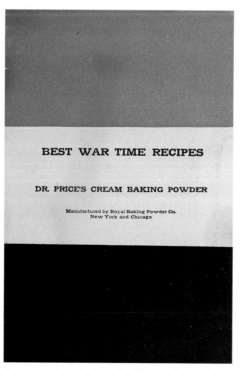

Best War Time Recipes, Dr. Prices Cream Baking Powder, 1918. Royal Baking Powder. 14 pages, 5" x 7.5". $15-$20.

Wheat Substitute Recipes, ca. 1918. Yeast Foam, The Northwestern Yeast Company. 3 page fold out, 3" x 5.5". $15-$20.

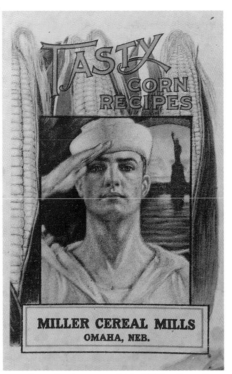

Tasty Corn Recipes, ca. 1918. Miller Cereal Mills. 6 pages, 3" x 4.5". $10-$15.

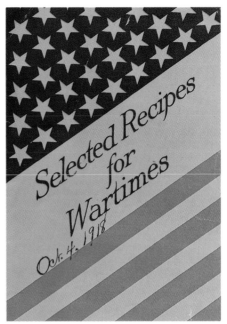

Selected Recipes for Wartimes, 1918. Calumet Baking Powder. 10 pages, 4.75" x 6.75". $15-$20.

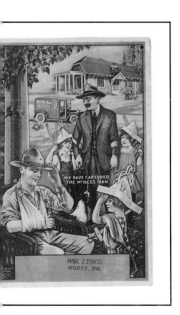

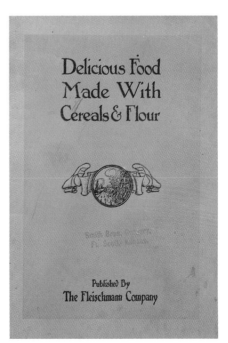

Recipes, War Breads, 1918. Dr. D. Jayne & Son. Considered more collectible among World War I collectors due to attractive cover. 32 pages, 3.5" x 6.25". $30-$40.

Delicous Food Made with Cereals & Flour, ca. 1918. The Fleischmann Company. Inside: "A Nation at War must be a Nation of Soldiers." 20 pages, 4.5" x 6.75". $10-$15.

WORLD WAR II

Between the years 1939-1945, advertising for World War II soared. The country's patriotism was high, men went to war, and the women of the country were called to do their part at the assembly line, farm, office, and volunteer work. As production of goods shifted to the war effort, many shortages were experienced. Automobiles were not being made and gasoline was rationed. Food items were rationed, such as sugar, butter, meat, eggs and cheese, among others. Using food efficiently and nutritionally for the family became a popular concern. Victory gardens, canning, and quick one-dish meals took priority, as cookbooks joined in the crusade to win the war.

Kerr Home Canning Book, 1943. Kerr Glass Manufacturing Corporation. 56 pages, 6.75" x 9.5". $10-$15.

Kate Smith Says: "Give 'em the home-baked treats they love!," 1945. General Foods Corporation. 15 pages, 4.25" x 4.5". $5-$10.

Meat in the Meal for Health Defense, 1942. National Live Stock and Meat Board. 40 pages, 5.25" x 8". $10-$15.

How to Hold Over Fruit for the Winter, 1943. The Great Western Sugar Company. 19 pages, 4" x 6.5". $5-$10.

Victory Cook Book, 1943. Lehn & Fink Products Corporation, Lysol. 32 pages, 5.5" x 8.5". $5-$10.

ressy Dishes from Your Victory Garden, 1945.
he Estate Stove Company. 16 pages, 5.5" x
25". $5-$10.

SWIFT & COMPANY
South St. Joseph, Missouri

Wartime Meat Recipe Book, Meat Point Pointers,
ca. 1940s. Swift & Company. 40 pages, 5.25" x
7.75". $15-$20.

dd Zest to War-Time Menus, ca. 1940s.
'alker's Austex Chili Company. 8 page fold
t, 4" x 5.75". $5-$10.

The Wartime Cook Book, 1942. Culinary Arts
Institute, Consolidated Book Publishers. 64
pages, 6" x 8.75". $15-$20.

Lunchtime on the Home Front, 1942. National
Dairy Council. "Mrs. America serves her
country." 7 pages, 5.5" x 8.5". $5-$10.

250 Ways to Save Sugar Cook Book, 1942. Culinary Arts Institute. 48 pages, 6" x 9". $10-$15.

Meat Recipe Book, Victory Meat Extenders, ca. 1940. National Live Stock and Meat Board. 40 pages, 5.25" x 7.75". $10-$15.

Cookies From Home for the Boys at Camp, Some Suggestions from Aunt Jenny, ca. 1940. Spry Shortening. 6 page fold out, 3.25" x 6". $5-$10.

Wartime Recipes From Canned Foods, ca. 1940. American Can Company. 26 pages, 6" x 9". $15-$20.

Victory Canning, 1942. Culinary Arts Institute. 64 pages, 7" x 9.75". $5-$10.

Chapter 9 Die-Cut Advertising Cookbooks

During the late 1800s and early 1900s, the printing industry developed a new technique for producing attractive books. First marking an outline of a product or illustration on wooden rollers, printers then inserted thin blades on the outline, which cut out shapes on paper. The end result was a recipe booklet that caught the consumer's attention, helped with product identification, and promoted sales.

Sleepy Eye Cook Book, 1904. Sleepy Eye Milling Company. Extremely rare. 96 pages, 5" x 4.5". $150-$165.

Aunt Jemima's Special Cake and Pastry Flour, 1906. Attractive die-cut recipe book, rare. 40 pages, 3.5" x 5". $175-$200.

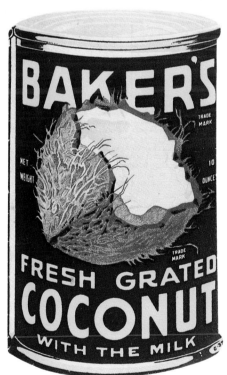

Baker's Fresh Grated Coconut with the Milk, ca. 1930s. 8 pages, 2.75" x 4.75". $20-$25.

It's All In the Jar, ca. 1903. Hazel-Atlas Glass Company. 20 pages, 3" x 6.25". $30-$35.

Wilbur's Cocoa, 1912. H. O. Wilbur & Sons. 8 pages, 3.75" x 4.5". $60-$70.

Dold's Hamper, ca. 1900. Jacob Dold Hams, The Jacob Dold Packing Company. 16 pages, 4.5" x 5". $40-$45.

Richard Hellmann's Blue Ribbon Mayonnaise,
1925. This unusual die-cut recipe book with
calendar and dial is difficult to find completely intact. Often, the unattached cookbook is mistakenly sold by itself. Richard
Hellman, Inc. 20 pages, 4.5" x 10". $50-$55.

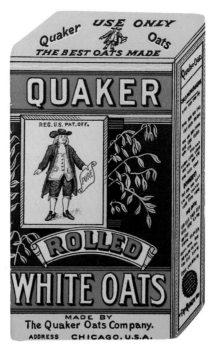

Quaker Rolled White Oats, ca. 1910s. The
Quaker Oats Company. 12 pages, 3.25" x 5.25".
$45-$50.

Cottolene, 1896. The N. K. Fairbank Company. Small advertising cookbook. 8 pages,
2.25" x 2.5". $40-$45.

Vegex Cook Book, ca. 1922. Vitamin Food
Company. 30 pages, 3.25" x 5.25". $10-$15.

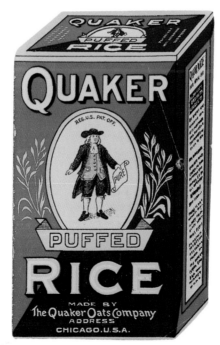

Quaker Puffed Rice, ca. 1910s. The Quaker Oats
Company. 8 pages, 3.25" x 5.25". $45-$50.

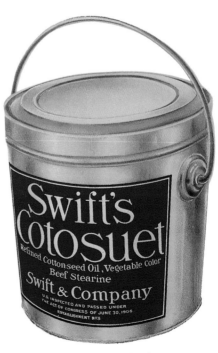

Swift's Cotosuet, ca. 1906. Swift & Company.
30 pages, 3.5" x 5". $35-$40.

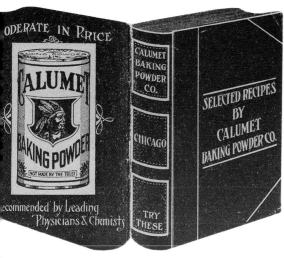

Selected Recipes by Calumet Baking Powder Company, ca. 1930's. 16 pages, 3.5" x 5.25". $25-$30.

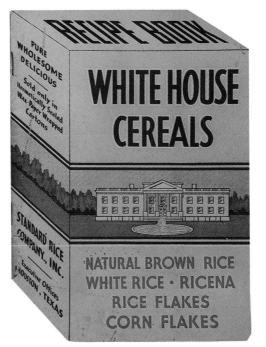

White House Cereals, ca. 1915. Standard Rice Company, Inc. 48 pages, 5" x 6.75". $15-$20.

Town Crier Ready Mixed Flour Recipes, ca. 1920s. Town Crier Food Products, Inc. 16 pages, 4" x 5.5". $25-$30.

King's Dehydrated Fruits and Vegetables, ca. 1915. Kings Food Products Company. 24 pages, 4.5" x 6.5". $20-$25.

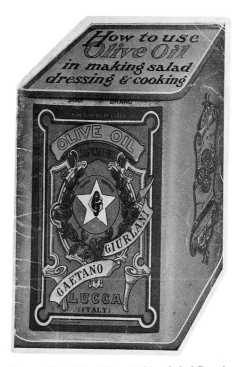

How to Use Olive Oil in Making Salad Dressing & Cooking, ca. 1920s. A. Giurlani & Brothers. 16 pages, 4.25" x 6.5". $20-$25.

Snowdrift, ca. 1925. The Wesson Oil & Snowdrift People. 3 page fold out, 4" x 5.25"; unfolded, 8" x 9.5". $10-$15.

Duff's Ginger Bread Mix made with Duff's Molasses, ca. 1930. 16 pages, 3.5" x 4.5". $10-$15.

Duff's Bran Muffin Mix made with Duff's Molasses, ca. 1930. P.D. Duff & Sons, Inc. 20 pages, 3.5" x 4.5". $10-$15.

Towle's Bucket Syrup, ca. 1930s. The Pioneer Maple Products Company. 2 page leaflet, 3" x 3.5". $15-$20.

Wesson Oil, ca. 1920. 4 page fold out, 3.25" x 6". $15-$20.

Portuguese Genuine Sardines Recipes, 1939. World's Fair Souvenir by The Portuguese Institute. 2 page fold out, 4" x 5". $10-$15.

Log Cabin Syrup Recipes, ca. 1930s. General Foods Corporation. 14 pages, 4.5" x 3.75". $25-$35.

Chapter 10 Black Memorabilia Cookbooks

Black Memorabilia continues to be highly collectible in any category, regardless of the type of item. These cookbooks portray all the Southern hospitality, wholesome spirit, and appealing culinary dishes that have made the Southern states famous throughout the world.

Missus - I Tole Yo dat Davis' No. 10 Flour do dat way!! ca. 1890. R. T. Davis Mill Company. pages unknown, rare, 5.5" x 8.5". $60-$75.

Once You Taste These Syrups You'll Ask For More Too, ca. 1930s. Mapleade Syrup, W. B. Roddenbery. 3 page fold out, 4" x 6". $15-$20.

Culinary Wrinkles, ca. 1900s. Armour's Extract of Beef, Armour and Company, considered rare. 32 pages, 4" x 5". $70-$85.

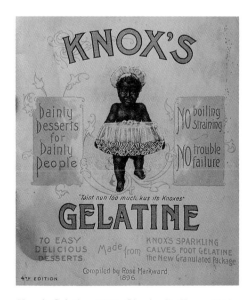

Snowdrift, ca. 1920s. Advertising die-cut. Popular among Black Memorabilia collectors. 4 page fold out, 3" x 6". $20-$25.

Snowdrift Secrets, 1912. The Southern Cotton Oil Company. Wonderful artwork, highly collectible among Black Memorabilia collectors. 48 pages, 5" x 7". $50-$70.

Knox's Gelatine, 1896. Charles B. Knox. This book was compiled by Mr. Knox's wife, Rose Markward. 32 pages, 5.25" x 6". $30-$40.

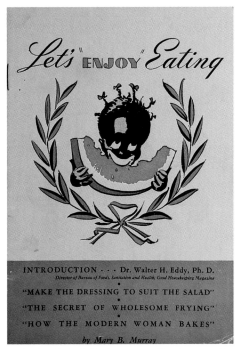

Let's "Enjoy" Eating, 1932. The Wesson Oil and Snowdrift People. 30 pages, 5" x 7.25". $20-$25.

Omega Flour Tested Recipes, ca. 1930s. Omega Flour Mills. 24 pages, 4" x 6". $15-$20.

A Recipe No Other Mammy Cook Could Equal, 1930. Aunt Jemima, Quaker Oats Company, 15 pages, 6" x 3". $60-$75.

Angostura Recipes, 1934. Angostura Bitters. 38 pages, 4.5" x 6". $20-$25.

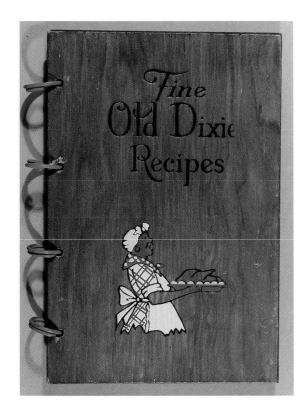

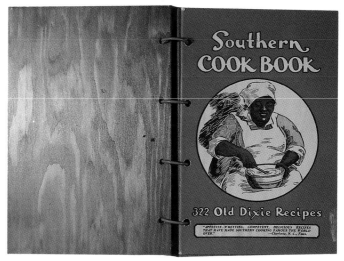

Southern Cook Book, 322 Old Dixie Recipes, 1939. Culinary Arts Press, wooden cover with plastic rings. This book was also published without the wooden cover and no three hole punches. 48 pages, 6.25" x 9.25". $35-$40.

New Orleans Recipes, 1932. Mary Moore Bremer. 90 pages, 5.5" x 7.75". $25-$30.

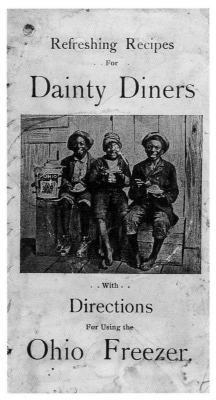

Refreshing Recipes for Dainty Diners, 1895. Ohio Freezer Company. 10 pages, 3.25" x 6". $45-$50.

Ice-Frozen Desserts, 1932. Evaporated Milk Association. 24 pages, 5.5" x 8.5". $25-$30.

Chapter 11 Media Promotions

Radio, television, and motion pictures played a large role in the distribution of cookbooks. Thousands were ordered by mail or bought for souvenirs to remember famous celebrities.

Every evening into America's living room entered the sights and sounds of favorite stars, comedians, variety shows, and music. Jack Benny and Mary Livingston were on the air for Jell-O, Fibber McGee and Molly were created for the Pet Milk Show, Kate Smith promoted Swan's Down Cake Flour, and Sarah and Aggie's Party Line peddled recipes and Dr. Caldwell's medicines. It was a time of food, fun, and entertainment.

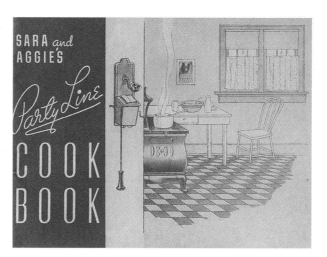

Sarah and Aggie's Party Line Cook Book Second Edition, 1936. Dr. W. B. Caldwell, Inc. 32 pages, 6" x 4.25". $10-$15.

Kate Smith's Favorite Recipes, 1940. General Foods Corporation. 48 pages, 7.75" x 9.5". $15-$20.

Sarah and Aggie's Party Line Cook Book, 1936. Dr. W. B. Caldwell, Inc. The "Tuttle" Family was introduced as a radio program to promote Syrup Pepsin, a liquid laxative invented by Dr. Caldwell. 32 pages, 4.75" x 6.75". $15-$20.

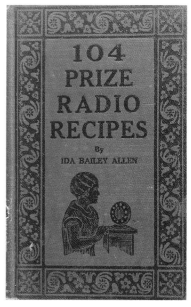

104 Prize Radio Recipes, 1926. Ida Bailey Allen was the founder of the National Radio Home-Maker's Club with "meetings" held over the radio for thousands of members. Hard cover, 125 pages, 4" x 6.5". $20-$25.

Gone With the Wind Cook Book, 1961. Metro-Goldwyn Mayer, Inc. Few motion pictures were as popular as the film classic *Gone With The Wind* in 1939. These recipes were inspired by characters such as Scarlett O'Hara and Aunt Pittypat. This issue was promoted as a limited edition by Colonial Stores. 48 pages, 5.5" x 7.75". $40-$45.

Jack & Mary's Jell-O Recipe Book, 1937. General Foods Corporation. Every Sunday evening Jack Benny, Mary Livingston, and Don Wilson entertained Americans over the radio air waves. At the beginning of each show, Jack would start with his famous introduction "Jell-O Again!" The show started in 1934 and continued for over ten years. 24 pages, 5.5" x 7.5". $15-$20.

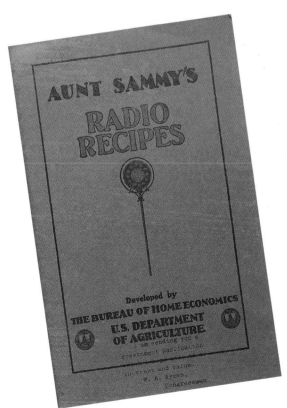

Aunt Sammy's Radio Recipes, ca. 1927. The Bureau of Home Economics, U. S. Department of Agriculture. "Housekeeper's Chats" was a popular radio series for women from October 1926 through June 1927. The U.S. Department of Agriculture produced the book due to the high demand for recipes (Aunt Sammy was Uncle Sam's wife). Many congressmen handed out the books free of charge. 86 pages, 6" x 9". $10-$15.

Chapter 12 Children's Themes

During the early years of the twentieth century, children's books not only flourished but also became a valuable advertising tool for the commercial food industry. Appealing to children, manufacturers could spread their name directly into the households of America. Printing and publishing techniques continued to improve and attract new talent with competition high to secure the best authors and writers. These books introduce the reader to a world of fantasy, magical and whimsical characters, and delightful scenery. A combination of puzzles, coloring books, tracing pamphlets, and stories became an enormous marketing success nationwide.

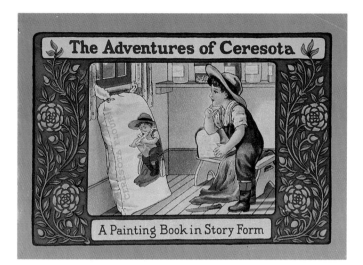

The Adventures of Ceresota, A Painting Book in Story Form, 1912. No recipes. Included concentrated paints on paper, highly collectible. 48 pages, 8" x 6". $55-$65.

The Little Gingerbread Man, 1923. Royal Baking Powder Company. 16 pages, 7.25" x 7.25". $30-$35.

Billy in Bunbury, 1925. Dr. Price's Baking Powder, Royal Baking Powder Company. 10 pages, 7" x 7". $15-$20.

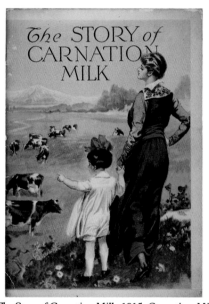

The Story of Carnation Milk, 1915. Carnation Milk Products Company. Claims their brand is the best because it comes from "contented cows." 32 pages, 5" x 7". $20-$25.

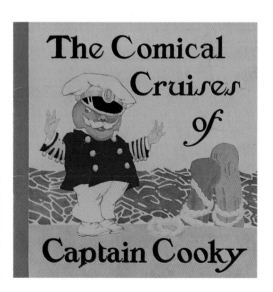

Left:
The Comical Cruises of Captain Cooky, 1926. Royal Baking Powder Company. 24 pages, 7" x 7". $30-$35.

Right:
Childrens' Party Book, 1935. A. E. Staley Manufacturing Company. 24 pages, 7.25" x 6.75". $15-$20.

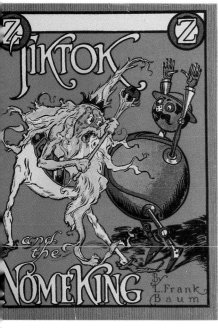

Tiktok and the Nome King, 1933-34. Frank L. Baum, The Reilly & Lee Company. This storybook includes Jell-O recipes and is highly collectible among *Wizard of Oz* collectors. 30 pages, 5" x 6.5". $100-$125.

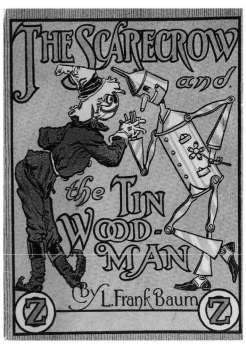

The Scarecrow and the Tin Wood-Man, 1933-34. Frank L. Baum, The Reilly & Lee Company. This storybook includes Jell-O recipes and is highly collectible among *Wizard of Oz* collectors. 30 pages, 5" x 6.5". $100-$125.

Jack Pumpkinhead and The Sawhorse, 1933-34. Frank L. Baum, The Reilly & Lee Company. This storybook includes Jell-O recipes and is highly collectible among *Wizard of Oz* collectors. 30 pages, 5" x 6.5". $100-$125.

This picture shows the back of these four *Wizard of Oz* booklets. There were duplicate books produced between the years 1933 and 1934 that did not include Jell-O recipes. For easy identification, just look for the keyhole image on the back of the books.

Ozma and the Little Wizard, 1933-34. Frank L. Baum, The Reilly & Lee Company. This storybook includes Jell-O recipes and is highly collectible among *Wizard of Oz* collectors. 30 pages, 5" x 6.5". $100-$125.

The Ad~ven~tur~ous Billy and Betty, 1923.
Van Camp Products Company. Illustrated
by Carl Mueller. 24 pages, 5.5" x 8.5".
$15-$20.

Little Stories for Little Children, 1885. Yeast Foam/
Magic Yeast, no recipes. 8 pages, 4.5" x 5.74".
$25-$30.

Untitled, Marvel Flour. 1916. Listman Mill
Company. Children's tracing book, no
recipes. 8 pages, 3.25" x 5". $15-$20.
Photo 15/19

Sunshine Magic Color Painting book, ca.
1920s. Sunshine Biscuits, Loose-Wiles
Biscuit Company, no recipes. This book
includes concentrated paint pallets - just
add water. 28 pages, 5" x 7". $15-$20.

The Talking Millstones, 1945. Pillsbury Mills,
Inc., no recipes. Illustrated by Henry C. Pitz
(1895-1976) who was well-known for over 160
illustrations in magazines, books, and contests.
78 pages, 6.75" x 9". $20-$25.

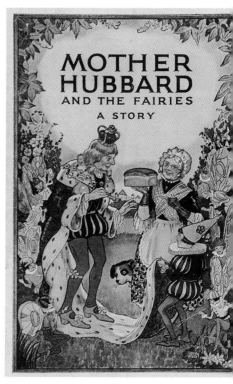

Mother Hubbard and the Fairies A Story, 1927.
Mother Hubbard Flour, nice illustrations.
Hubbard Milling Company. 12 pages, 5" x
7.5" . $25-$30.

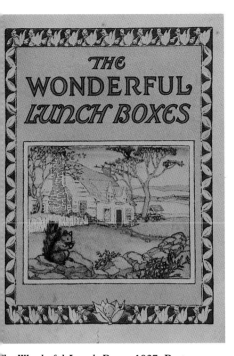

The Wonderful Lunch Boxes, 1927. Postum Company, Inc., no recipes. 16 pages, 4" x 5.5". 10-$15.

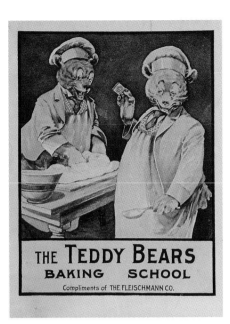

The Teddy Bears Baking School, 1906-1907. The Fleischmann Company, no recipes. 12 pages, 5" x 6.5". $40-$45.

Fleischmann's Jingles, 1905. The Fleischmann Company, no recipes. 12 pages, 4.75" x 6.5". $25-$30.

Hidden Treasure, 1927. Postum Company, Inc., no recipes. 8 pages, 4.5" x 6.5". $10-$15.

Easy Drawing for Little Ones, 1902. The Fleischmann Company, no recipes. 8 pages, 3" x 5". $25-$30.

Untitled, Fleischmann's Yeast, ca. 1900s. The Fleischmann Company. Tracing book, no recipes. 8 pages, 3" x 5". $15-$20.

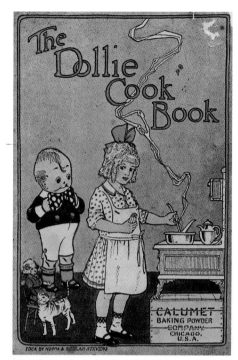

The Dollie Cook Book, 1916. Calumet Baking Powder Company. Illustrated by R. D. Streng, included easy recipes for children. 12 pages, 4" x 6". $25-$30.

The Children's Party Book, 1923. Calumet Baking Powder. Artist Frances Tipton Hunter (1896-1957) illustrated this book, as well as many other children's illustrations. 40 pages, 6.5" x 8". $50-$60.

Kellogg's Funny Jungleland Moving-Pictures, 1909. W. K. Kellogg, no recipes. 3 page fold out with moving characters, 6" x 8". $25-$30.

Kellogg's Funny Jungleland Moving-Pictures, 1932. Kellogg's, no recipes. 3 page fold out with moving characters, 6" x 8". $25-$30.

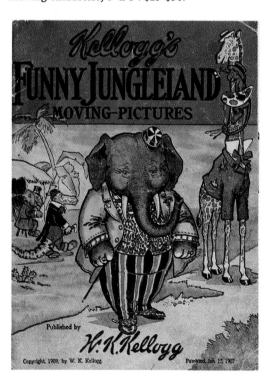

Here is an inside view of these Kellogg's Jungleland children's books.

Mickey Mouse Recipe Scrap Book, ca. 1930s. Gold Cup Bread, Walt Disney Enterprises. This was a promotional advertising book which was given away in Gold Cup Bread packages. Various pictures were collected by children to paste in this book. Popular among Disney collectors. 48 pages, 4.25" x 6.25". $75-$85.

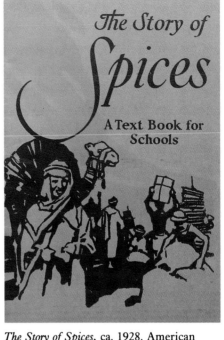

The Story of Spices, ca. 1928. American Spice Trade Association, no recipes. This book was produced as a text book for schools. 15 pages, 4.75" x 7". $5-$10.

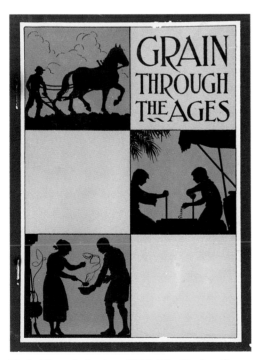

Grain Through the Ages, 1929. The Quaker Oats Company, no recipes. Illustrated by Jessie Gillespie and published for elementary schools. 96 pages, 5.25" x 7.25". $15-20.

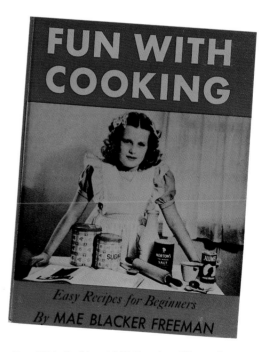

Fun With Cooking, 1947. Random House, Inc., hard cover. 58 pages, 8" x 10.25". $10-$15.

Chapter 13 Publications

Many housewives enjoyed the pleasure of having recipe books arrive at their doorstep. To promote their subscriptions, publishers produced annual cookbooks which were offered through the mail.

AMERICAN TRADE COUNCIL

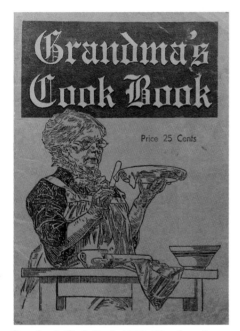

Grandma's Cook Book, 1932. The American Trade Council. 94 pages, 7.5" x 10.5". $10-$15.

CULINARY ARTS PRESS

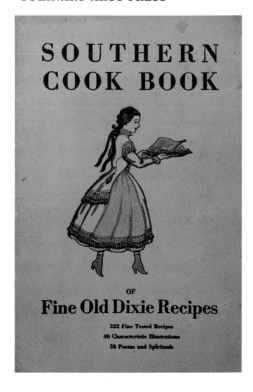

Pennsylvania Dutch Book, Fine Old Recipes, 1936. Culinary Arts Press. 48 pages, 6.25" x 9.25". $15-$20.

Left:
Southern Cook Book, 1935. Culinary Arts Press. 48 pages, 6" x 9". $15-$20.

Old Pennsylvania Dutch Recipes, 1936. Culinary Arts Press. This book is identical to the *Pennsylvania Dutch Book.* It was published with a wooden cover and plastic rings. 48 pages, 6.25" x 9.25". $25-$35.

Left:
Fine Old New England Recipes, 1936. Culinary Arts Press. This book is identical to the *New England Cook Book* shown below. It was published with a wooden cover and plastic rings. 48 pages, 6.25" x 9.25". $25-$35.

New England Cook Book, 300 Fine Old Recipes, 1936. 6"x 9". $25-$35.

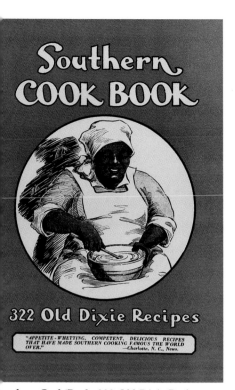

Southern Cook Book, 322 Old Dixie Recipes, 1939. Culinary Arts Press. 48 pages, 6.25" x 25". $35-$40.

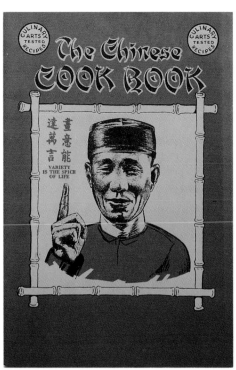

The Chinese Cook Book, 1936. Culinary Arts Press. 47 pages, 6" x 9". $10-$15.

Quick Dinners for the Woman in a Hurry Cook Book, 1942. Culinary Arts Institute. 48 pages, 6" x 9". $10-$15.

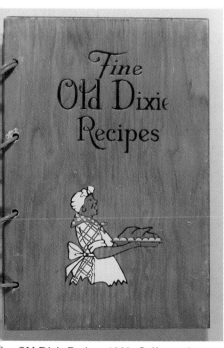

Fine Old Dixie Recipes, 1939. Culinary Arts Press. This book is identical to the Southern Cook Book. It was published with a wooden cover and plastic rings. 48 pages, 6.25" x 25". $35-$45.

2,000 Useful Facts About Food, 1941. Culinary Arts Institute. 48 pages, 6" x 8.75". $10-$15.

FARM AND FIRESIDE LIBRARY

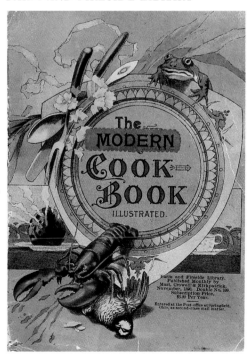

The Modern Cook Book, ca. 1890s. Farm and Fireside Library, Mast Crowell & Kirkpatrick. For three dollars, customers could receive a monthly subscription to these books for one year. 320 pages, 5.25" x 7.25". $30-$35.

PHILADELPHIA INQUIRER

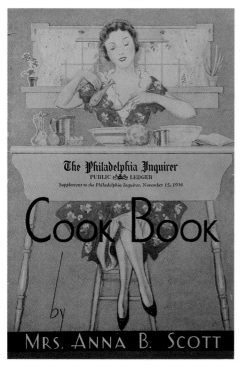

The Philadelphia Inquirer Cook Book, 1936. This was a supplement to the newspaper on November 15, 1936. 32 pages, 6" x 9". $10-$15.

Priscilla Helps for Housekeepers, ca. 1915. The Priscilla Publishing Company. 45 pages, 7.75" x 10.5". $20-$25.

WOMAN'S WORLD MAGAZINE

Woman's World Cookery Calendar, 1922. Woman's World Magazine Company, Inc. 66 pages, 7" x 10.25". $10-$15.

PRISCILLA MAGAZINE

Priscilla Cook Book for Everyday Housekeepers, 1913. Edited by Fannie Merritt Farmer, The Priscilla Publishing Company. 48 pages, 7.75" x 10.5". $20-$25.

REVIEW & HERALD PUBLISHING

Better Meals for Less, 1930. Review & Herald Publishing. 128 pages, 5.25" x 7.75". $10-$15

The Fifty Two Sunday Dinners, 1927. Woman's World Magazine Company, Inc. 66 pages, 6.75" x 10". $10-$15.

COOKERY CALENDAR

Being a selection of tested recipes for every month and properly balanced menus based on nutrition and economy, with cooking time tables for exact results.

ORIGINATED AND PUBLISHED BY
WOMAN'S WORLD MAGAZINE CO. INC.
CHICAGO, U.S.A.

Cookery Calendar, 1927. Woman's World Magazine Company, Inc. 50 pages, 6.75" x 10". $10-$15.

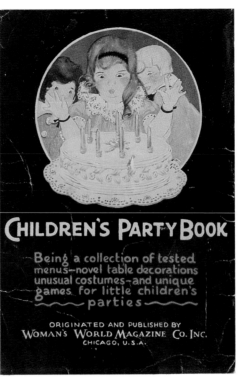

CHILDREN'S PARTY BOOK

Being a collection of tested menus–novel table decorations unusual costumes–and unique games for little children's parties

ORIGINATED AND PUBLISHED BY
WOMAN'S WORLD MAGAZINE CO. INC.
CHICAGO, U.S.A.

Children's Party Book, 1928. Woman's World Magazine Company, Inc. 50 pages, 6.75" x 10". $10-$15.

UNION PACIFIC RAILROAD

150 Recipes for Apple Dishes issued by Agricultural Department Union Pacific System Omaha, Nebraska

150 Recipes for Apple Dishes, 1924. Union Pacific System. 38 pages, 5.5" x 8.75". $10-$15.

FISH BOOK

Being a collection of tested recipes of fresh and salt water fish–featuring the practical and appetizing ways of its preparation cooking and service

ORIGINATED AND PUBLISHED BY
WOMAN'S WORLD MAGAZINE CO. INC.
CHICAGO, U.S.A.

Fish Book, 1928. Woman's World Magazine Company, Inc. 50 pages, 6.75" x 10". $10-$15.

THE BOOK OF COOKERY

The American Housewife Collection of Tested Menus and Recipes-Appetizing & Practical

The Book of Cookery, 1931. Manning Publishing Company, The Woman's World Service Library. 58 pages, 10.25" x 13.75". $10-$15.

Chapter 14 Culinary Authors

Many authors both famous and unknown published cookbooks in the culinary field. Some of the more prominent included Fannie Merritt Farmer, Eliza Leslie, Sarah Tyson Rorer, Catherine Beecher, and Marion Harland. They included topics such as cooking techniques, catering, fund raising, housekeeping, health tips, and caring for children. A majority of these hard cover books were elaborately illustrated and included endorsements for products.

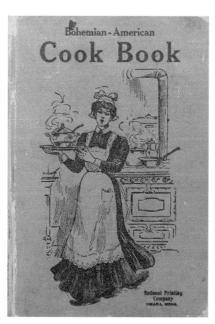

Bohemian-American Cook Book, 1915. Mary Rosicky, hard cover. Published in Bohemian and English languages. 307 pages, 5.25" x 7.75". $20-$25.

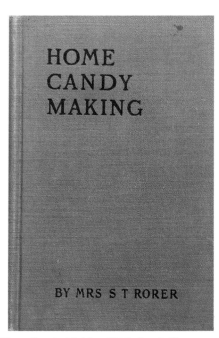

Home Candy Making, 1911. Sarah Tyson (Heston) Rorer (1847-1937) was the famous author of at least forty cookbooks. She was considered a culinary expert at The Philadelphia School of Domestic Science, and was also the Domestic Editor of the *Ladies Home Journal* until 1911. Hard cover, 89 pages, 5" x 7.5". $85-$90.

Catering for Special Occasions with Menus & Recipes, 1911. Fannie Merritt Farmer, (1857-1915) also authored *The Boston Cooking School Cook Book.* This book contains beautiful illustrations by Albert D. Blashfield with cherub figures on each page. 240 pages, 5.5" x 8". $75-$80.

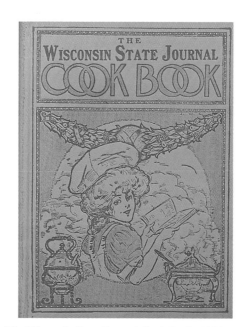

The Wisconsin State Journal Cook Book, 1908. Emma Paddock Telford, The Wisconsin State Journal, hard cover. 254 pages, 5.5" x 7.5". $40-$45.

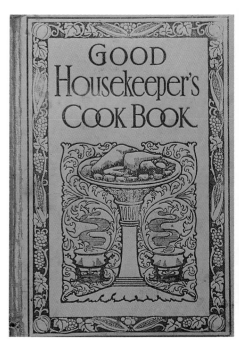

Good Housekeeper's Cook Book, 1914. Emma Paddock Telford, hard cover. 256 pages, 6.25" x 8.75". $40-$45.

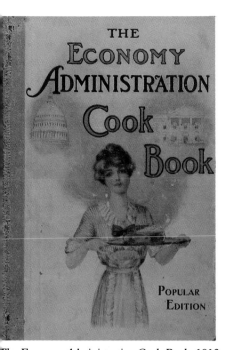

The Economy Administration Cook Book, 1913. Susie Root Rhodes and Grace Porter Hopkins. Recipes were contributed by famous diplomats, senators, and congressmen in the United States Government. 322 pages, 5.5" x 7.75". $55-$65.

Woman's Favorite Cook Book, 1902. Anne R. Gregory, hard cover. This book contains three volumes in one, with colorful drawings and photo engravings. 578 pages, 7.5" x 9.5". $65-$70.

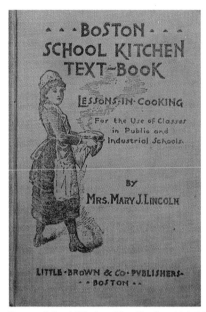

Boston School Kitchen Text-Book, 1914. Mrs. Mary Lincoln, hard cover. 237 pages, 5" x 7.25". $20-$30.

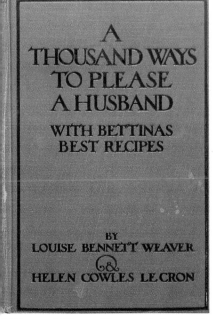

A Thousand Ways to Please a Husband with Bettina's Best Recipes, 1917. Louise Bennett Weaver and Helen Cowles LeCron, hard cover. 479 pages, 5.5" x 8". $45-$55.

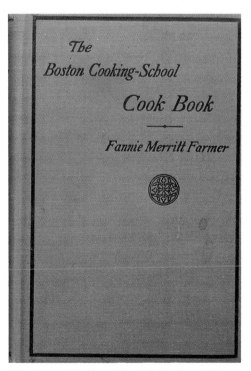

The Boston Cooking School Cook Book, 1919. Fannie Merritt Farmer and Mary W. Farmer, hard cover. 656 pages, 5.25" x 7". $25-$35.

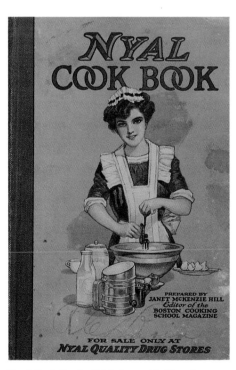

Nyal Cook Book, 1916. Janet McKenzie Hill, The Boston Cooking-School Magazine Company, hard cover. This book was only available at Nyal Drug Stores. 224 pages, 5.25" x 7.5". $50-$60.

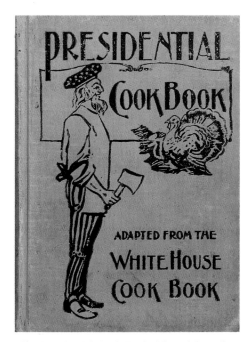

The Presidential Cook Book Adapted from the White House Cook Book, 1907. Hugo Ziemann and Mrs. F. L. Gillette, Saalfield Publishing Company, hard cover. This was a condensed version of *The White House Cook Book* and included a photo of Mrs. Edith Carew Roosevelt. 440 pages, 6.25" x 8.5". $35-$45.

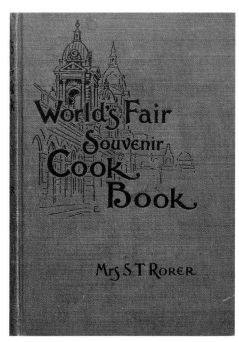

World's Fair Souvenir Cook Book, 1904. Mrs. Sarah Tyson Rorer, hard cover. This was a souvenir of the Louisiana Purchase Exposition World's Fair in St. Louis, Missouri. 202 pages, 5.5" x 7.75". $100-$125.

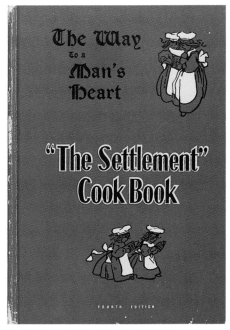

The Settlement Cook Book, The Way to a Man's Heart, 1910. Mrs. Simon Kander, The American Crayon Company, hard cover. This book was produced by Mrs. Simon Kander (Lizzie Black 1858-1940) of the Milwaukee Jewish Mission. She requested $18.00 from the Board of Directors to publish a fund raiser cookbook and was refused. The members of the church then self-published the book through local advertisers. They raised enough funds to build a new settlement house building, and the book sold over a half million copies in seventy-five years. 453 pages, 5.5" x 7.5". $65-$75.

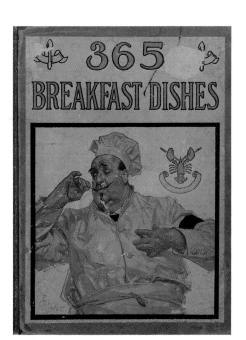

365 Breakfast Dishes, 1901. George W. Jacobs and Company, hard cover. 169 pages, 5" x 7". $40-$45.

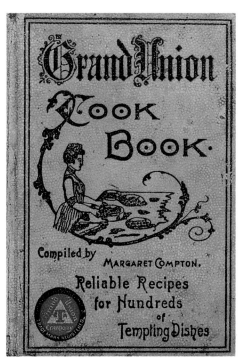

Grand Union Cook Book, 1902. Margaret Compton, Grand Union Tea Company, hard cover. 322 pages, 5.25" x 7.75". $45-$50.

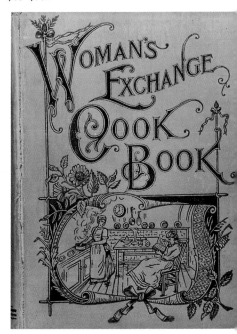

Woman's Exchange Cook Book, 1901. Mrs. Minnie Palmer, hard cover, nice illustrations. 527 pages, 7.5" x 9.75". $60-$75.

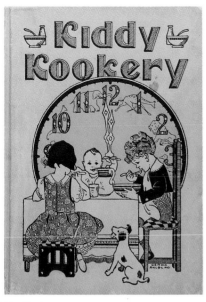

Kiddy Kookery, 1923. Leah Barash Kahn, Kiddy Kookery Publishing Company, hard cover. This book gave advice and recipes for raising children from infants to six years old, illustrations by Ruth Kreps. 92 pages, 5.5" x 5". $10-$15.

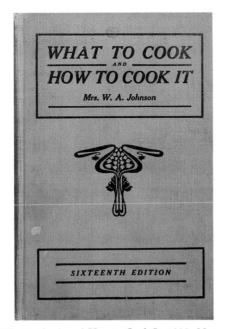

What to Cook and How to Cook It, 1899. Mrs. W. A. Johnson, hard cover. 291 pages, 5.25" x 7.75". $35-$40.

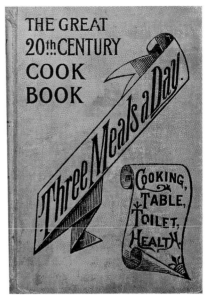

The Great 20th Century Cook Book - Three Meals a Day, 1890. Maud C. Cooke, hard cover. 576 pages, 6.5" x 9.25". $60-$65.

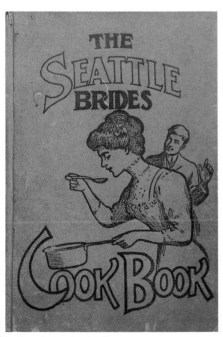

The Seattle Brides Cook Book, ca. 1900. The Union Advertising Company, hard cover. Provides recipes and advertisements from local dealers to new brides of Seattle, Washington. 122 pages, 7" x 10.25". $35-$40.

Health Foods and How to Prepare Them, 1899. Emma Todd Anderson, National Institute of Science, hard cover. 228 pages, 5.5" x 8". $40-$45.

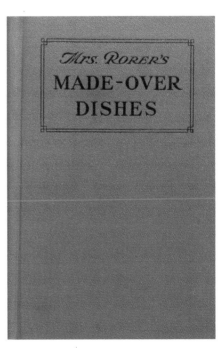

Made-Over Dishes, 1912. Mrs. Sarah Tyson Rorer, hard cover. 110 pages, 5" x 7.5". $45-$50.

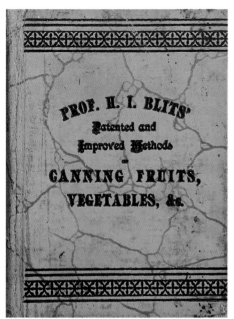

Professor H. I. Blits' Patented and Improved Methods of Canning Fruits, Vegetables, Etc., 1890. H. I. Blits, hard cover. 523 pages, 6" x 8". $40-$45.

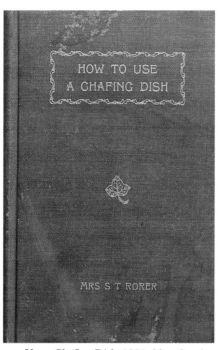

How to Use a Chafing Dish, 1894. Mrs. Sarah Tyson Rorer, hard cover. 73 pages, 3.25" x 5.75". $75-$85.

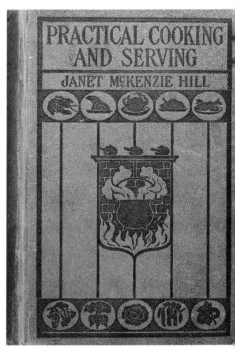

Practical Cooking and Serving, 1908. Janet McKenzie Hill, hard cover. Hill was also the author of *The Boston Cooking School Magazine.* 731 pages, 5.75" x 8.25". $35-$45.

La Bonne Cuisine, 1929. Madame E. Staint-Ange, Librarie Larousse-Paris, hard cover. This book was published in French and has many illustrations. 448 pages, 4.5" x 7". $35-$40.

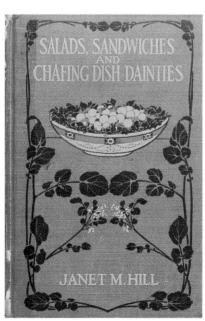

Salads, Sandwiches and Chafing Dish Dainties, 1919. Janet McKenzie Hill was a famous author and lecturer who was hired by numerous companies such as Rumford, Kerr, Jell-O, Cottolene, and Plymouth Rock Gelatine. Hard cover, 231 pages, 5" x 7.5". $35-$40.

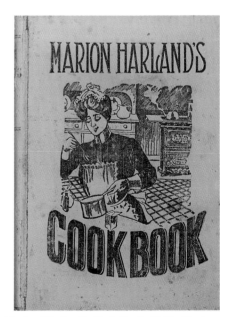

Marion Harland's Cook Book, 1907. Marion Harland, hard cover. 157 pages, 5.5" x 7.5". $25-$35.

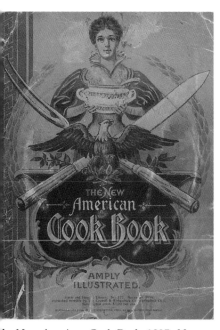

he New American Cook Book, 1897. Mast, rowell, & Kirkpatrick. Recipes were conibuted by chefs and famous culinary artists ich as Sarah Tyson Rorer, the chef for the /hite House, Paul Resel, and many more. 33 pages, 5.75" x 8". $45-$50.

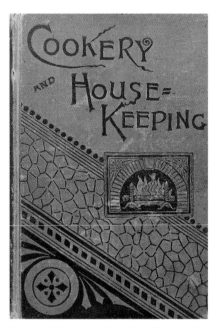

Cookery and Housekeeping, By a Veteran Housekeeper, 1886. Published by M. T. Richardson, hard cover. Many authors in the late 1800s wished to remain anonymous and requested their names not be identified in the publication. 473 pages, 5.25" x 7.75". $40-$45.

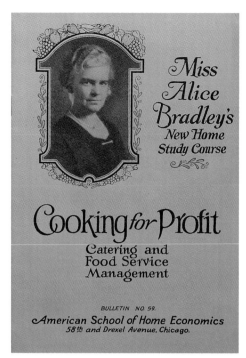

Miss Alice Bradley's New Home Study Course, Cooking for Profit, 1927. American School of Home Economics. 15 pages, 5.25" x 7.5". $10-$15.

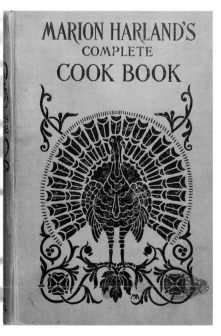

arion Harland's Complete Cook Book, 1906. arion Harland (1830-1922) was the author f many cookbooks and publications. She as hired by many companies such as Kerr, ottolene, Jell-O, and Corn Products Refin- ig Company who made Argo, Karo, and lazola Oil. 781 pages, hard cover, 6" x 8.5". 45-$50.

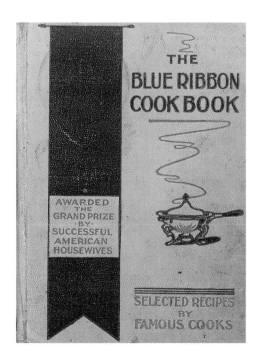

The Blue Ribbon Cook Book - Selected Recipes by Famous Cooks, 1907. Anne R. Gregory, hard cover. This book contains wonderful illustrations and photo engravings. 580 pages, 7.5" x 9". $80-$85.

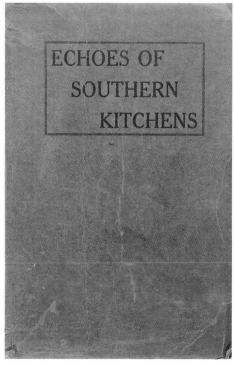

Echoes Of Southern Kitchens, 1916. United Daughters of the Confederacy. This book was a fund raiser and included General Robert E. Lee's favorite meat and vegetable dish. 94 pages, 6" x 8.75". $20-$25.

How to Use Olive Butter, 1883. Mrs. S. T. Rorer, Washington Butcher's Sons. 20 pages, 3.25" x 5.5". $20-$30.

The Calendar of Luncheons, ca. 1920s. Elizabeth O. Hiller. This recipe calendar came packaged in an attractive gift box. 60 pages, 5.5" x 11". $25-$30.

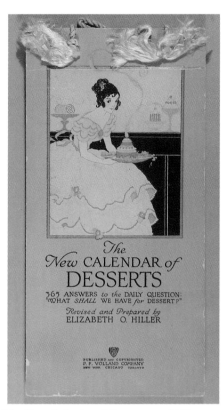

The New Calendar of Desserts, ca. 1920. Elizabeth O. Hiller. This recipe calendar came packaged in an attractive gift box. 60 pages, 5.5" x 11". $25-$30.

The Calendar of Sandwiches & Beverages, ca. 1920s. This recipe calendar came packaged in an attractive gift box. 60 pages, 5.5" x 11". $25-$30.

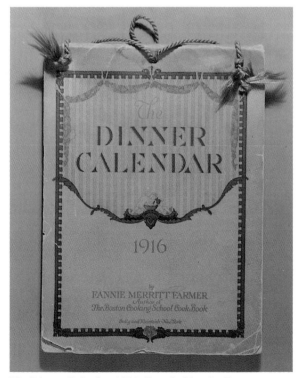

The Dinner Calendar, 1916. Fannie Merritt Farmer, top clasp book. 56 pages, 7" x 9.5". $30-$35.

Chapter 15 Medicines, Tonics, & Life Insurance

One of the more entertaining aspects of collecting cookbooks is the category of medicine guides and almanacs. In the past, business was welcomed in the rural back roads of our country where transportation was limited. Doctors, pharmacists, and even enterprising housewives with an herb or medicine formula to sell entered the profession. Traveling by horse and buggy, they sold their products door-to-door providing antidotes, testimonials, and recipes in their books. Insurance salesmen also provided complimentary copies of recipes when they called to collect premiums. Topics included cures for liver complaints, impure blood, whooping cough and carbuncles. Recipes such as Mrs. H's Boiled Batter Pudding, Oyster Fritters and even Mock Turtle soup were included. The same medicines could even cure your horse, cattle, and chickens!

CARDUI

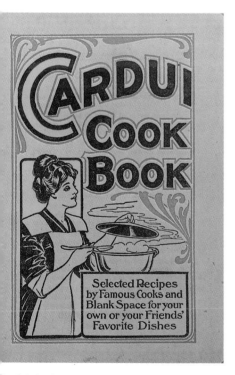

Cardui Cook Book, 1912. Cardui Tonic, Chattanooga Medicine Company. 24 pages, 5" x 7.25". $10-$15.

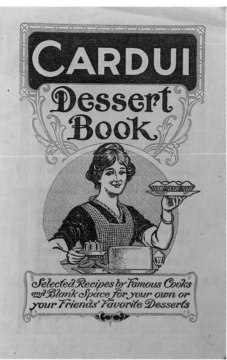

Cardui Dessert Book, 1914. Cardui Tonic, Chattanooga Medicine Company. 24 pages, 5" x 7.25". $10-$15.

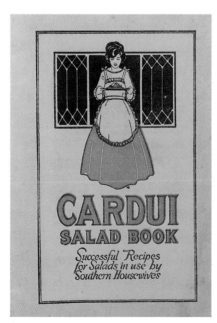

Cardui Salad Book, 1923. Cardui Tonic, Chattanooga Medicine Company. 22 pages, 5 x 7.25". $10-$15.

DR. CALDWELL'S

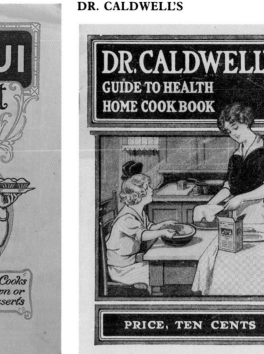

Dr. Caldwell's Guide to Health Home Cook Book, ca. 1905. Pepsin Syrup Company. 33 pages, 4.75" x 6.75". $10-$15.

Dr. Caldwell's Guide to Health Home Cookbook, ca. 1906. Pepsin Syrup Company. 33 pages, 4.75" x 6.75". $10-$15.

DR. FENNER'S

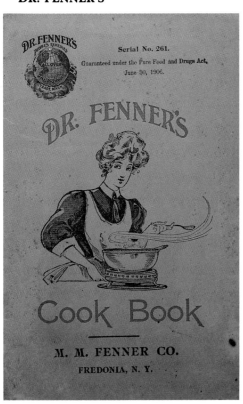

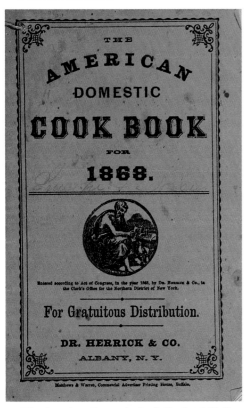

DR. JAYNE'S

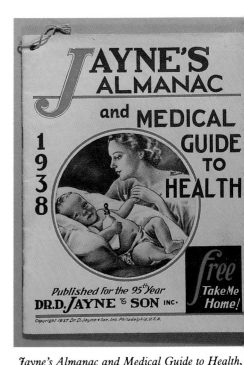

Dr. Fenner's Cook Book, 1906. M. M. Fenner Company. 31 pages, 5.5" x 8.5". $10-$15.

Recipes, War Breads, 1918. Dr. D. Jayne & Son. Considered highly collectible among World War I collectors due to attractive cover. 32 pages, 3.5" x 6.25". $30-$40.

Jayne's Almanac and Medical Guide to Health, 1937. Dr. D. Jayne & Son, Inc. 32 pages, 5.5" x 7". $10-$15.

DR. HERRICK'S

DR. KING'S

The American Domestic Cook Book, 1868. Dr. Herrick & Company. 32 pages, 6" x 4.5". $30-$35.

Jayne's New Canning Book, 1936. Dr. D. Jayne & Son, Inc. 32 pages, 3.5" x 6". $10-$15.

Dr. King's New Beauty Book Health Guide Cook Book, 1904. H. E. Bucklen & Co. 32 pages, 6.5" x 9". $15-$20.

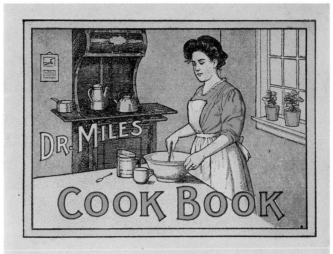

Dr. Miles' Cook Book, 1919. 33 pages, 6.25" x 5". $5-$10.

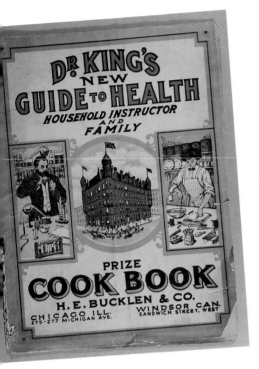

r. King's New Guide to Health Household Instructor nd Family Cook Book, 1910. 32 pages, 6.75" x 9". 15-$20.

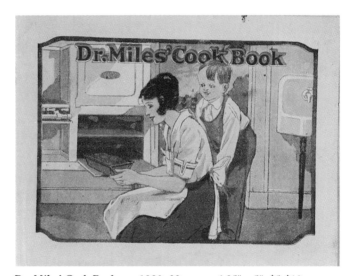

Dr. Miles' Cook Book, ca. 1920. 33 pages, 6.35" x 5". $5-$10.

DR. MILES'

DR. PIERCE'S

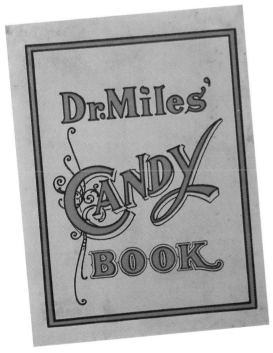

Neighborhood Gossip Dream Book, ca. 1910s. V. M. Pierce, M. D. 32 pages, 5.5" x 4". $5-$10.

Dr. Miles' Candy Book, 1910. Miles Medical Company. 34 pages, 4.75" x 6.25". $5-$10.

145

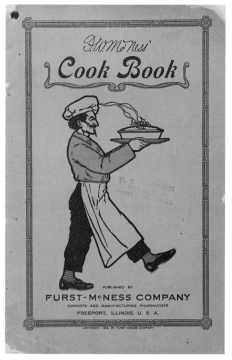

F. W. McNess Cook Book, 1908. Furst-McNess Company. 32 pages, 6" x 9". $10-$15.

F. W. McNess Cook Book, ca. 1920s. Furst-McNess Company. 64 pages, 6" x 9". $10-$15.

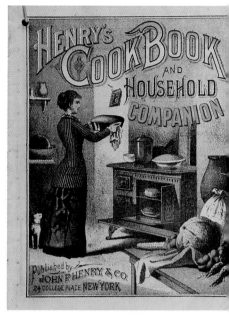

Henry's Cook Book and Household Companion, 1881. John F. Henry & Company. 32 pages, 5" x 6.5". $25-$30.

LYDIA PINKHAM

The McNess Cook Book, ca. 1918. Furst-McNess Company. 32 pages, 5.75" x 8.5". $15-$20.

F. W. McNess' Cook Book, ca. 1930s. Furst-McNess Company. 32 pages, 6" x 9". $10-$15.

When hard times hit her family in 1873, Lydia E. Pinkham did not despair. Fortunately, she had been making and selling her herbal medicine for years and saw it as an opportunity to capitalize on the business. Lydia often sold a few bottles of her medicine, made to cure "female complaints," to neighbors in Lynn, Massachusetts. It wasn't until a party of ladies from Salem drove up to her house and bought half a dozen bottles for five dollars that she finally realized its full potential.

The original formula called for a collection of roots and herbs with the mixture suspended in approximately 19 percent alcohol. Lydia brewed the compound on a stove in the cellar while her sons, Dan and Will, handed out pamphlets and sold the product door-to-door.

Sales grew slowly until 1881, when Dan ingenuously applied his mother's picture to the label. Her image, highly composed in her best black silk and lace dress, seemed to confirm the creditability of the product. Profits soared and so did Lydia's popularity. Her face adorned newspapers, magazines, and drugstore displays. Even college glee clubs, fascinated with her image, wrote songs and verses, further increasing sales.

Sadly, the Pinkhams did not live to enjoy their fortune. Dan and Will both died of pneumonia in the fall of 1881 and Lydia died two years later at the age of sixty-four. The business remained in the hands of the surviving children, reaching an annual sales volume of $3 million in 1925.

Stretching Your Dollar, 1930s. Lydia E. Pinkham Medicine Company. 32 pages, 4.5" x 7". $5-$10.

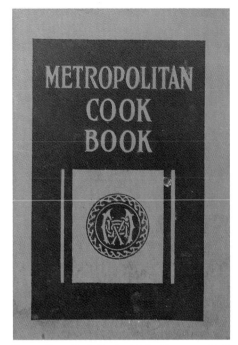

Metropolitan Cook Book, 1922. 64 pages, 5.25" x 7.75". $5-$10.

Come into the Kitchen, ca. 1920s. Lydia E. Pinkham Medicine Company. 32 pages, 4.5" x 7". $5-$10.

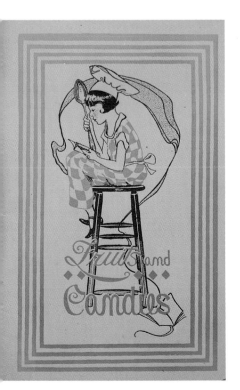

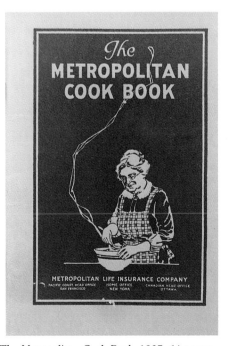

Favorite Recipes, ca. 1930s. Lydia E. Pinkham Medicine Company. 32 pages, 4.5" x 7". $5-$10.

The Metropolitan Cook Book, 1927. 64 pages, 5.25" x 7.5". $5-$10.

Fruits and Candies, ca. 1930s. Lydia E. Pinkham Medicine Company. 32 pages, 4.5" x 7". $5-$10.

The Metropolitan Cook Book, 1935. 64 pages, 5.25" x 7.5". $5-$10.

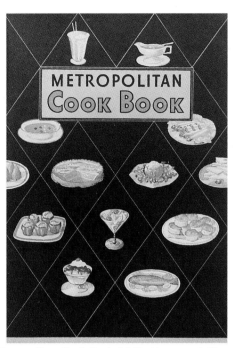

Good Stories and Recipes, 1901. Nature's Remedy, A. H. Lewis Medicine Company. 24 pages, 3.5" x 5.75". $5-$10.

Meteropolitan Cook Book, 1942. 64 pages, 5.5" x 7.75". $5-$10.

PARACAMPH

MRS. WINSLOW'S

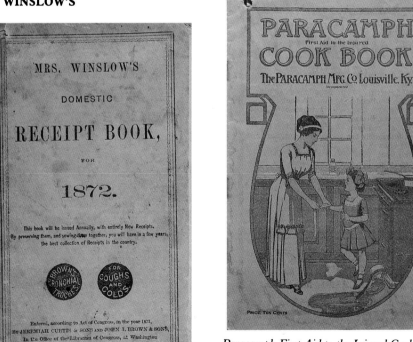

The Family Food Supply, 1940. 23 pages, 5.25" x 7.75". $5-$10.

Mrs. Winslow's Domestic Receipt Book, 1872. Jeremiah Curtis & Sons and John I. Brown & Sons. 32 pages, 4" x 6.25". $30-$35.

Paracamph First Aid to the Injured Cook Book, ca. 1911. The Paracamph Mfg. Company. 32 pages, 6" x 8.5". $10-$15.

Prudential Cook Book and Household Hints, ca. 1904. Prudential Insurance Company. 32 pages, 4" x 5.75". $25-$30.

RANSOM'S

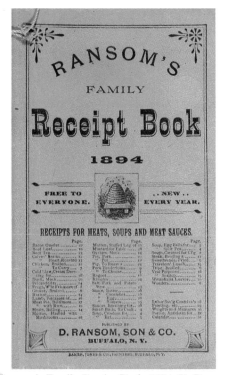

Ransom's Family Receipt Book, 1894. D. Ransom, Son & Company. 32 pages, 4" x 6.5". $20-$25.

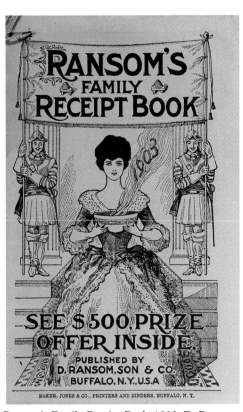

Ransom's Family Receipt Book, 1903. D. Ransom, Son & Company. 32 pages, 4" x 6.5". $15-$20.

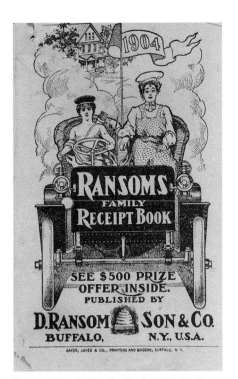

Ransoms Family Receipt Book, 1904. D. Ransom, Son & Company. 32 pages, 4" x 6.5". $15-$20.

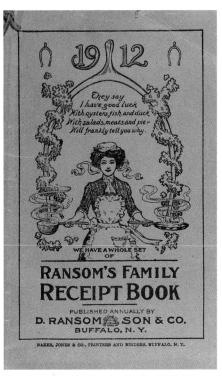

Ransom's Family Receipt Book, 1912. D. Ransom, Son & Company. 32 pages, 4" x 6.5". $15-$20.

Ransom's Family Receipt Book, 1915. D. Ransom, Son & Company. 32 pages, 4" x 6.5". $15-$20.

RAWLEIGH'S PRODUCTS

It was in 1889 that young W.T. Rawleigh rode to the state line of Illinois in a horse and wagon and called on his first customer's home. With just a sample case he turned a vision into a thriving business. This was a time when telephones and electricity were new, street cars were drawn by horses, and the primary source for delivery was on dusty roads. Since there were limited hospitals and doctors, housewives relied on homemade remedies such as goose grease and onion syrup to keep their families well. Rawleigh's Good Health Products were a welcome addition. By 1895, a rented factory was started with three employees. Within a year, thirty men were retailing the company's products and by 1898 the first factory was built in Freeport, Illinois. Its continued popularity, growth, and service developed the Rawleigh Industries into the huge international company it is today.

Rawleigh's Almanac Cook Book & Medical Guide, 1911. 64 pages, 5.75" x 8.75". $10-$15.

Rawleigh's Good Health Guide Almanac Cook Book, 1921. 64 pages, 6.5" x 9.5". $10-$15.

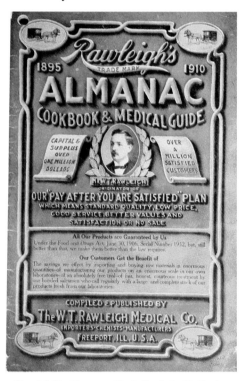

Rawleigh's Almanac Cook Book & Medical Guide, 1910. W. T. Rawleigh Medical Company. 64 pages, 6" x 8.75". $10-$15.

Rawleigh's Almanac Cook book & Medical Guide, 1915. 100 pages, 5.75" x 8.75". $10-$15.

Rawleigh's Good Health Guide and Cook Book, 1928. 32 pages, 6.5" x 9.25". $10-$15.

Sloan's Handy Hints and Up-To-Date Cook Book, 1901. Sloans Liniment, Dr. Earl S. Sloan. 48 pages, 4.5" x 6.5". $15-$20.

WATKIN'S

Joseph R. Watkins was a young man of twenty-eight when he decided to enter the world of business. In 1868, he purchased from Dr. Richard Ward of Cincinnati, Ohio the rights to manufacture and sell various liniments and medicines the doctor had been using in his practice. The young entrepreneur started producing, bottling, and selling the products with a new concept in mind: to bring them directly to the customer's door. He began with horse and buggy, traveling through the local towns and villages. As demand for his products increased, he added new dealers which made him more successful throughout the Midwest. By 1885, headquarters were established in Winona, Minnesota. Later, branch offices were established throughout the United States and international markets were opened by 1915. The J.R. Watkins Company was well on its way to enjoying world-wide distribution and ultimate success

Watkins' Kalender, 1904. The J. R. Watkins Medical Company, German version. 94 pages, 6" x 9". $15-$20.

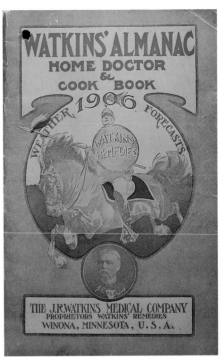

Watkin's Almanac Home Doctor & Cook Book, 1906. 96 pages, 6" x 9". $15-$20.

Watkins Flavoring Extracts, ca. 1916. 32 pages, 4.5" x 8". $15-$20.

Better Baking, ca. 1920s. 16 pages, 8" x 5". $10-$15.

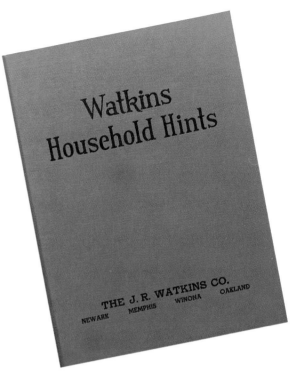

Watkin's Household Hints, 1941. J. R. Watkin's Company. Hard cover spiral. 272 pages, 6.5" x 8.5". $15-$20.

WORLD DISPENSARY

The Ladies Note-Book and Calendar, 1887. World's Dispensary Medical Association. 24 pages, 3.5" x 5.75". $10-$15.

Better Baking, ca. 1920s. 16 pages, 8" x 5". $10-$15.

Chapter 16 Cookware, Products, & Appliances

Kitchen equipment and appliances changed dramatically through the years as new technology made the housewife's duties in the kitchen easier and more pleasant. Cookbooks show us an array of products such oil stoves, fireless cookers, electric refrigerators, canning supplies, serving utensils, and hand-cranked ice cream freezers. Companies continued to keep pace with the future by adapting and revising their products and recipes to reflect this new period of growth. They provide us a with visual history of how life in the kitchen has changed.

20th CENTURY FREEZER

Ices Dainty and Novel, ca. 1900s. 20th Century Freezer, Cordley & Nayes. 32 pages, 3.5" x 6.25". $15-$20.

ACORN STOVES

Thirty Dainty Dishes and Acorn All-Cast Ranges, ca. 1905. Acorn Stoves, Rathbone, Sard & Company. 14 pages, 5" x 6.5". $10-$15.

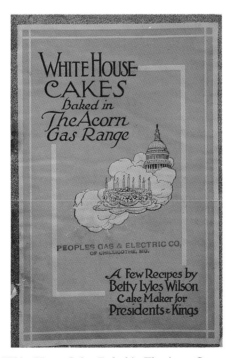

White House Cakes Baked in The Acorn Gas Range, ca. 1913. Rathbone, Sard, & Company. 21 pages, 5" x 7.5". $10-$15.

ARMSTRONG TABLE COOKER

Table Cookery The Armstrong Way, 1919. Armstrong Manufacturing Company. 31 pages, 5" x 7". $10-$15.

AUTO VACUUM FREEZER

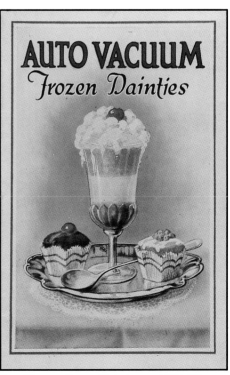

Auto Vacuum Frozen Dainties, ca. 1910. The Auto Vacuum Freezer Company, Inc. 32 pages, 4.5" x 6.75". $10-$15.

BALL GLASS

It was fast action on the part of William Charles Ball and his brothers Lucius, Frank, Edmund, and George that started them on their way to a lucrative business in 1887. The Ball Brothers Manufacturing Company had been making tin-jacked glass containers for kerosene lamps since 1880, but Thomas Edison's invention of the new incandescent light bulb was soon to make their product obsolete. They discovered a patent which had expired for a reusable screw-type canning jar. The Mason jar was the invention of John Landis Mason, a Brooklyn, New York metalworker, in 1857. It consisted of a molded thread in a glass jar top with a zinc lid that had a threaded ring sealer. Manufacturing of their former product made it easy to shift to the new fruit jars and lids. Since Mason's patent had moved into public domain, the brothers started production in 1887 in their new facilities located in Buffalo, New York. By the end of the first year, they had produced 12,500 containers with the new name "Ball" impressed into the glass jars. Headquartered in Muncie, Indiana, the Ball Corporation still continues to make one of the highest quality brands of canning equipment sold in America today.

The Ball Blue Book of Canning and Preserving Recipes, 1915. Ball Brothers Glass Manufacturing Company. 79 pages, 5.25" x 8.25". $15-$20.

CLUB ALUMINUM WARE

The Recipe Book for Club Aluminum Ware, 1925. Club Aluminum Company. 30 pages, 5.75" x 8.75". $10-$15.

DANA FREEZER

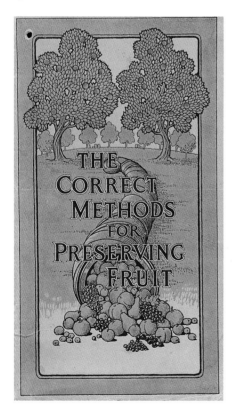

The Correct Methods for Preserving Fruit, ca. 1910. 31 pages, 5" x 9". $35-$40.

How to Use the Foods You Can, 1924. 41 pages, 5.25" x 7.25". $10-$15.

Ice Cream and Ices by Well-Known Cooks, ca. 1890s. Dana Peerless Freezer, The Dana Mfg. Company. 24 pages, 3.75" x 5.75". $15-$20.

Fireless Cooking, ca. 1910. Durham Manufacturing. 48 pages, 5" x 6.5". $15-$20.

The Enterprising Housekeeper, 1897. The Enterprise Manufacturing Company. 80 pages, 4.5" x 6.75". $25-$30. *Courtesy of James Welsh, Jr.*

The Enterprising Housekeeper, 200 Tested Recipes, 1906. 96 pages, 5" x 7". $25-$30.

The Enterprising Housekeeper, 200 Tested Recipes, 1900. 80 pages, 4.5" x 6.5". $25-$30.

The Enterprising Housekeeper, 200 Tested Recipes, 1902. 94 pages, 4.5" x 6.5". $25-$30.

The Enterprising Housekeeper, 200 Tested Recipes, 1906. 96 pages, 5" x 7". $25-$30.

FLORENCE STOVES

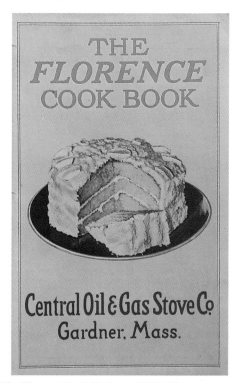

Frigidaire

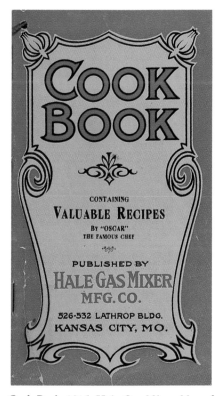

Enterprising Housekeeper, 200 Tested Recipes,
1913. 96 pages, 4.75" x 7". $25-$30.

EXCELSIOR STOVES

The Florence Cook Book, ca. 1921. Florence
Stoves, Central Oil & Gas Stove Company. The
inside of this book was identical to the 1921
New Dr. Price's Baking Powder Cook Book and
also the *New Royal Baking Powder Cook Book.*
50 pages, 5" x 8". $15-$20.

Frigidaire Advanced Refrigeration, 1931.
Frigidaire Corporation. 32 pages, 6" x 9".
$15-$20.

HALE GAS MIXER

*Assured Satisfaction Cooking and Useful
Recipes,* ca. 1917. Excelsior Stove & Mfg.
Company. 64 pages, 3.5" x 6.5". $10-$15.

FRIGIDAIRE REFRIGERATORS

Cook Book, 1915. Hale Gas Mixer Manufacturing Company. 32 pages, 3.5" x 6". $5-$10.

Frigidaire Frozen Delights, 1927. Frigidaire
Corporation. 48 pages, 4.75" x 7.25".
$15-$20.

HOME COMFORT RANGES

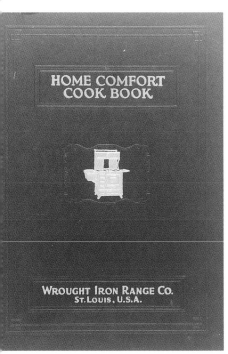

Home Comfort Cook Book, ca. 1934. Wrought Iron Range Company. This book features wonderful photographs of how ranges changed through the years. 212 pages, 6.25" x 9.75". $25-$30.

IDEAL FOOD CUTTER

The Ideal Receipt Book, 1898. Ideal Food Cutter, The Peck, Stow & Wilcox Company. 64 pages, 4" x 5.5". $30-$35.

JEWEL STOVES

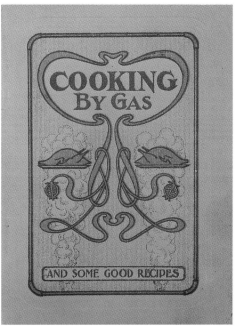

Cooking by Gas, ca. 1901. Jewel Stoves and Ranges, Detroit Stove Works. Contains recipes from Sarah Tyson Rorer, Marion Harland, and more! 95 pages, 4.5" x 6". $20-$25.

HUGHES STOVES

Perfected Electric Cooking, 1914. Hughes Electric Heating Company. 24 pages, 3.25" x 6". $10-$15.

IDEAL STEAM COOKER

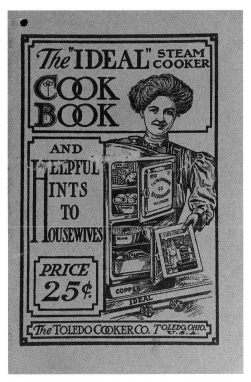

The Ideal Steam Cooker Cook Book, 1907. The Toledo Cooker Company. 88 pages, 5.25" x 7.75". $10-$15.

JEWEL TEA PRODUCTS

Starting a business with only a horse, a wagon, a little cash, and a lot of determination is just what Frank V. Skiff needed to be successful. In 1899, in Chicago, Illinois, he began buying what he thought the average housewife needed in the way of daily supplies, such as coffee, tea, spices, and extracts, and selling them door-to-door. By 1901, he had joined in a partnership with his brother-in-law, Frank P. Ross. They rented a small store and called their business The Jewel Tea Company, manufacturing their own brands of products. They served over a million customers by 1916. Mrs. Mary Hartson became the official Mary Dunbar spokesperson for Jewel Tea in 1924. (Dunbar was actually her maiden name.) She was responsible for establishing the Jewel Homemaker's Institute, which corresponded with customers on tips and recipes and published a newsletter. The Jewel Tea Company offered personal service along with quality merchandise premiums which remain highly collectible today.

476 Tested Recipes by Mary Dunbar, ca. 1926. Jewel Tea Company, Inc. 80 pages, 5.5" x 8.5". $5-$10.

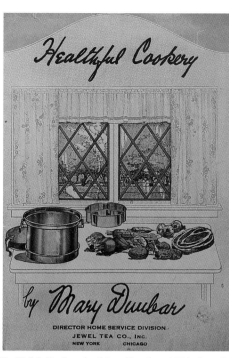

Healthful Cookery by Mary Dunbar, 1929. Jewel Tea Company, Inc. 23 pages, 4.75" x 6.75". $5-$10.

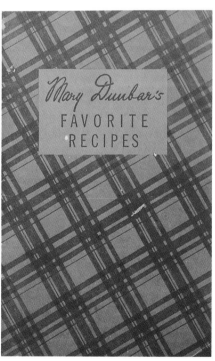

Mary Dunbar's Favorite Recipes, 1936. Jewel Tea Company, Inc. 80 pages, 5.25" x 9.5". $5-$10.

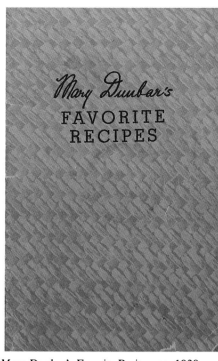

Mary Dunbar's Favorite Recipes, ca. 1938. Jewel Tea Company, Inc. 80 pages, 5.25" x 8.25". $5-$10.

KERR GLASS

Alexander Hewitt Kerr, from Portland, Oregon, was the first to introduce a metal lacquered screw-on lid for canning jars with an attached air-tight sealing gasket in the ring top in 1903. By 1915, Kerr moved his successful company to Sands Springs, Oklahoma.

Recipes for Home Canning in The Economy Airtight Jar, 1910. Kerr Glass Manufacturing Company. 30 pages, 3.25" x 8.5". $10-$15.

Kerr Home Canning Book, ca. 1930s. Kerr Glass Manufacturing Company. 48 pages, 5" x ?". $5-$10.

LORAIN STOVES

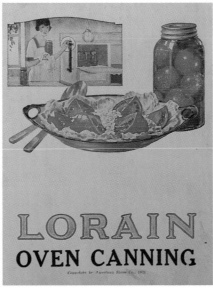

Lorain Oven Canning, 1921. Lorain Stoves, American Stove Company. 4 page fold out, 5.25" x 7.5". $5-$10.

Majestic Cook Book, ca. 1890s. 88 pages, 6" x 8.75". $20-$25.

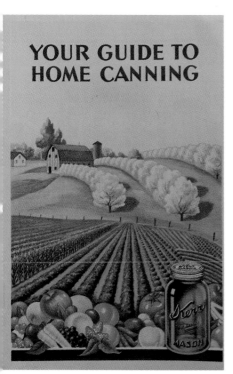

Your Guide to Home Canning, 1938. Kerr Glass Manufacturing Company. 12 pages, 4" x 6". $5-$10.

Strawberry Shortcake, 1925. Lorain Stoves, National Stove Company. 2 page leaflet, 4" x 9". $5-$10.

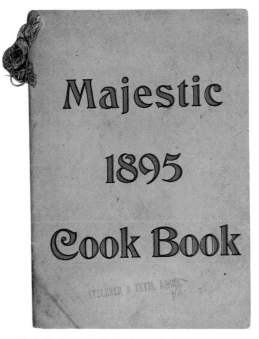

Majestic 1895 Cook Book, 1895. 56 pages, 4.75" x 6.75". $20-$25.

Majestic Cook Book, ca. 1899. 94 pages, 5" x 6.75". $20-$25.

Inside Range Information, ca. 1900s. The Malleable Steel Range Mfg. Company. 16 pages, 3.5" x 6.25". $10-$15.

Kitchen Economy Comfort Cooking, 1907. The Malleable Steel Range Mfg. Company. 80 pages, 3.75" x 8.5". $20-$25.

The Great Majestic Range Cook Book, ca. 1906. 96 pages, 7.75" x 10.75". $25-$30.

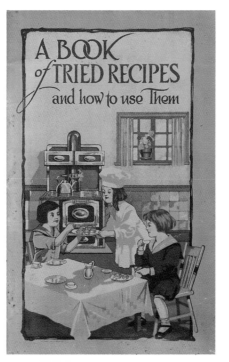

A Book of Tried Recipes and How to Use Them, ca. 1900s. Malleable Range, Engman-Matthews Range Company. 64 pages, 5" x 8". $20-$25.

Cook Book, 1907. 79 pages, 3.75" x 8.75". $20-$25.

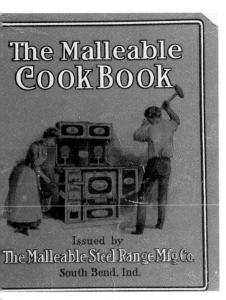

he Malleable Cook Book, ca. 1910. 80 pages,
.25" x 6.25". $20-$25.

*The All-ways Preferable Cook Book of The
South Bend Malleable Range,* ca. 1910. 96
pages, 4" x 7.25". $20-$25.

MIRRO ALUMINUM BAKEWARE

*What's New in Cookery From the Mirro Test
Kitchen,* 1929. Aluminum Goods Manufacturing Company. 30 pages, 5.25" x 6.75".
$10-$15.

MANNING & BOWMAN CHAFING DISH

'ook Book, ca. 1910. 64 pages, 4" x 5.5".
.20-$25.

*The Chafing Dish, Manning-
Bowman Tested Recipes,* ca.
1900s. 32 pages, 7" x 5".
$10-$15.

The Chafing Dish, ca. 1900s.
Manning-Bowman. 32 pages,
6.75"x 5". $10-$15.

Food Surprises from The Mirro Test Kitchen, ca. 1930s. Aluminum Goods Manufacturing Company. 16 pages, 4.5" x 6". $10-$15.

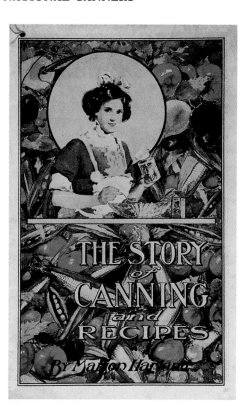

Eclipse Chopper Cook Book, ca. 1920s. Montgomery Ward & Company. 30 pages, 4.5" x 6.75". $10-$15.

NATIONAL CANNERS

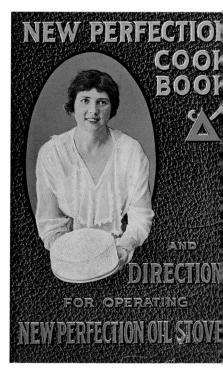

New Perfection Cook Book, ca. 1900s. New Perfection Oil Stoves. 96 pages, 5" x 7.25". $25-$30.

Finest Baking with Mirro The Finest Aluminum, ca. 1930s. Aluminum Goods Manufacturing Company. 4 page fold out, 3.25" x 6". $10-$15.

The Story of Canning and Recipes, 1910. Written by Marion Harland, National Canners Association. 40 pages, 5" x 8". $15-$20.

New Perfection Oil Cook-Stove, ca. 1910. Standard Oil Company. 19 pages, 3.5" x 6". $10-$15.

New Perfection Cook-Book, ca. 1910. The
Cleveland Foundry Company. 72 pages, 5" x
7". $25-$30.

New Perfection Cook-Book, 1916. The Cleveland Foundry Company. 96 pages, 5" x 7.25".
$25-$30.

Favorite Menus and Recipes of Six Famous
Cooks, 1928. The Perfection Stove Company.
60 pages, 4.5" x 6.5". $10-$15.

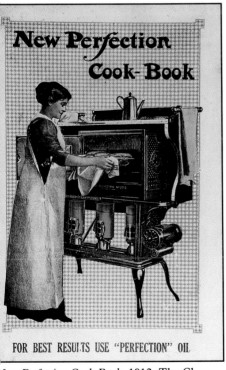

New Perfection Cook-Book, 1912. The Cleveland Foundry Company. 72 pages, 5" x 7.5".
$25-$30.

Directions and Cook Book, 1922. The Cleveland Metal Products Company. 68 pages,
4.75" x 7". $10-$15.

NORTH BROTHERS FREEZERS

Dainty Dishes For All The Year Round, 1897.
Mrs. S. T. Rorer, North Brothers Mfg. Co. 64
pages, 4.25" x 6.75". $15-$20.

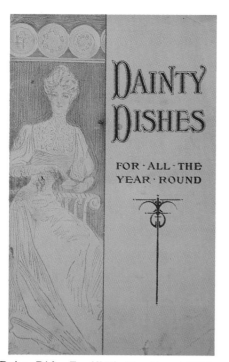

Dainty Dishes For All The Year Round, 1914. North Brothers Freezer, North Brothers Mfg. Company. Wonderful photos of mother and daughter preparing ice cream. 64 pages, 4.25" x 6.75". $15-$20.

Modern Household Helps, 1926. Standard Oil Company. 32 pages, 4.25" x 7.75". $15-$20.

PAR-O-WAX

The Parowax Book of Preserves, ca. 1926. Standard Oil Company. 32 pages, 4.25" x 7.75". $10-$15.

PYREX COOKWARE

There is a tale of Bavarian Prince Rupert who approached Charles II of England. He placed before him a small drop of glass the size and shape of a tadpole. He then hammered it squarely on the thick torso. It did not shatter or break after several attempts.

Experts Book on Better Cooking, 1925. Pyrex, Corning Glass Works. 28 pages, 6" x 9". $10-$15.

Then he gently flicked the thin tail of the tadpole and it shattered into tiny fragments. King Charles reportedly thought that Prince Rupert had performed witchcraft before his own eyes. Corning Glass Works understood Rupert's secret, that when a drop of glass was plunged into cold water, it would yield great strength.

The name originated in 1915 as a trademark for heat-proof baking dishes made of glass. The first suggestion was "Pie Right," but since they had other products ending in "x," they chose the name "Pyrex."

Complete Meals That Cook in 20 Minutes, 1930. Pyrex, Corning Glass Works. 16 pages, 5" x 7". $10-$15.

ROCHESTER COOKWARE

Serving Dish Receipts, ca. 1890s. Rochester Metal Mounted Earthenware, Rochester Stamping Company. 32 pages, 4.5" x 6.5". $20-$25.

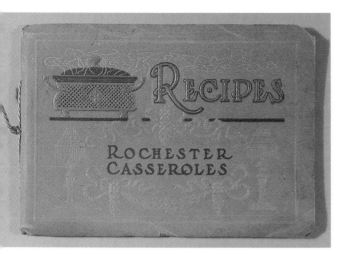

ecipes Rochester Casseroles, ca. 1900s. Rochester Metal Mounted arthenware, Rochester Stamping Company. 32 pages, 6" x 4.25". 20-$25.

OSETTE PATTY IRONS

Rosette" Wafers & Patties, 1905. Rosette Patty rons, Alfred Andresen & Company, nice llustrations. 20 pages, 2.75" x 4". $15-$20.

AVORY COOKWARE

Savory Prize Recipe Book, 1913. Highly collectible. 48 pages, 4" x 9". $60-$70.

Savory Better Living for Less Money, 1911. Highly collectible. 8 pages, 3" x 4.25". $50-$60.

Savory Prize Recipe Book for the "Savory" Roaster, 1922. Highly collectible. 48 pages, 3.5" x 6". $40-$50.

SEARS, ROEBUCK, AND COMPANY

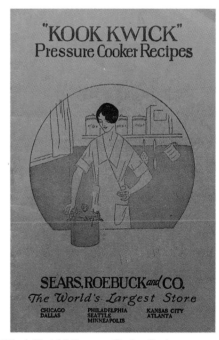

"Kook Kwick" Pressure Cooker Recipes, ca. 1940s. Sears, Roebuck and Company. 32 pages, 6" x 9". $5-$10.

SERV-EL REFRIGERATORS

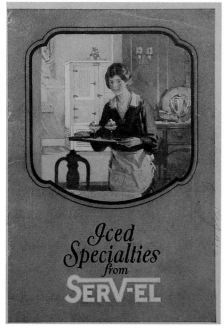

Iced Specialties from Serv-El, ca. 1930s.
Serv-el Corporation. 22 pages, 4.5" x 6.5".
$10-$15.

UNIVERSAL BREAD MAKER

Universal Bread Maker, ca. 1900s. Landers,
Frary & Clark. 12 pages, 3.5" x 6.25". $10-$15.

UNIVERSAL BROILER

A New Field of Cookery Broiled Foods, ca.
1930s. Universal In-A-Drawer Broiler,
Cribben & Sexton Company. 32 pages, 5" x
7.75". $10-$15.

SKELGAS

The Automaticook Book, 1927. Robert Shaw
& Herdstat Company. 58 pages, 6.75" x 10".
$5-$10.

The "Universal" Bread Maker, ca. 1904. Landers,
Frary & Clark. 16 pages, 3.5" x 6". $10-$15.

WEAR-EVER ALUMINUM

Canning Preserving & Jelly Making, ca. 1901. The Aluminum Cooking Utensil Company. 24 pages, 3.5" x 6". $15-$20.

The "Wear-Ever" Kitchen, ca. 1901. The Aluminum Cooking Utensil Company. 16 pages, 3.5" x 6". $15-$20.

Delicious Waffles, ca. 1915. Wagner Ware, The Wagner Manufacturing Company. Highly collectible. 4 pages, 3"x 4". $40-$45.

The inside of *The "Wear-Ever" Kitchen* cookbook shown above, has a wonderful illustration of a model kitchen during the early 1900s.

Healthful Foods, The New Method of Cooking, 1925. Wear-Ever, The Aluminum Cooking Utensil Company. 24 pages, 6" x 9". $10-$15.

The "Wear-Ever" New Method of Cooking,
1928. The Aluminum Cooking Utensil
Company. 48 pages, 6" x 9". $10-$15.

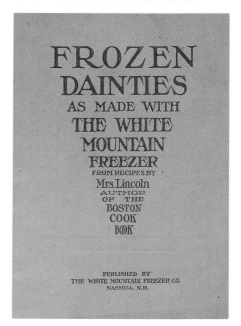

*Frozen Dainties as Made with The White
Mountain Freezer,* ca. 1890s. Written by Mary
J. Lincoln, The White Mountain Freezer
Company. 32 pages, 4.25" x 6". $20-$25.

WEST BEND COOKER

The Waterless Cooker Recipe Book, 1927. West Bend Aluminum Company.
These two books are identical with the exception of the cover - one is illustrated by an artist. 23 pages, 4" x 6.75". $5-$10.

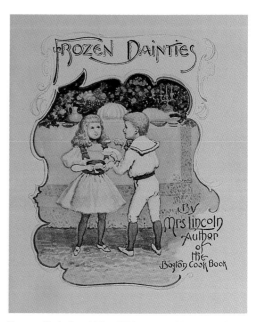

Frozen Dainties, 1897. Written by Mary J. Lincoln, The White Mountain Freezer Company.
Beautiful illustrations throughout. 32 pages,
4.5" x 5.75". $55-$60.

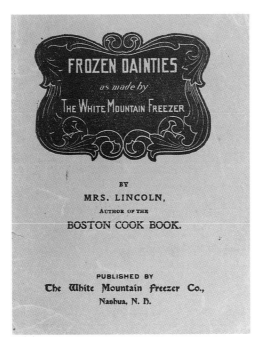

Frozen Dainties as Made With The White Mountain Freezer, 1898. Written by Mary J. Lincoln, The White Mountain Freezer Company. 32 pages, 4.5" x 5.75". $15-$20.

Frosty Fancies, 1898. Written by Mary J. Lincoln, The White Mountain Freezer Company. 16 pages, 5.75" x 4.5". $20-$25.

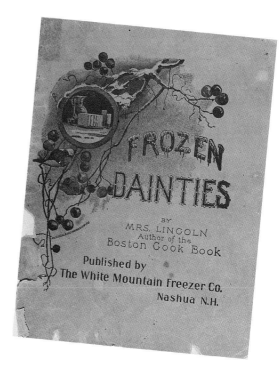

Frozen Dainties, 1902. Written by Mary J. Lincoln, The White Mountain Freezer Company. 31 pages, 4.5" x 5.75". $15-$20.

Bibliography

Allen, Col. Bob. *A Guide to Collecting Cookbooks and Advertising Cookbooks.* Paducah, Kentucky: Collector Books, A Division of Schroeder Publishing Company, Inc., 1995.

Barile, Mary. *Cookbooks Worth Collecting.* Radnor, Pennsylvania: Wallace-Homestead Book Company, A Division of Chilton Book Company, 1994.

Campbell, Hannah. *Why Did They Name It...?* New York, New York: Ace Books, A Division of Grosset & Dunlap, Inc., 1964.

Cleary, David P. *Great American Brands: The Success Formulas that Made Them Famous.* New York, New York: Fairchild Publications, A Division of Capital Cities Media, Inc., 1981.

DuSablon, Mary A. *America's Collectible Cookbooks.* Athens, Ohio: Ohio University Press, 1994.

Fritsche, L. A., M. D. *History of Brown County Minnesota: Its People, Industries and Institutions.* Indianapolis, Indiana: B. F. Bowen & Company, 1916.

Friz, Richard. *The Official Price Guide to World's Fair Memorabilia.* New York, New York: The House of Collectibles, 1989.

Fucini, Joseph J. and Suzy Fucini. *Entrepreneurs, The Men and Women Behind Famous Brand Names and How They Made It.* Boston, Massachusetts: G. K. Hall & Company, 1985.

Godcharles, Frederic A., Litt. D. *Chronicles of Central Pennsylvania.* New York, New York: Lewis Historical Publishing Company, Inc., 1944.

Gilbert, Anne. *The Official Price Guide American Illustrator Art.* New York, New York: House of Collectibles, 1991.

Grenier, Mildred. *St. Joseph A Pictorial History.* Virgina Beach, Virginia: the Donning Company/Publishers, 1981.

Hake, Ted. *Hake's Guide to Advertising Collectibles: 100 Years of Advertising From 100 Famous Companies.* Radnor, Pennsylvania: Wallace-Homestead Book Company, 1992

Hambleton, Ronald. *The Branding of America.* Dublin, New Hampshire: Yankee Publishing Incorporated, 1987.

Hammond, Dorothy. *Advertising Collectibles of Times Past.* Des Moines, Iowa: Wallace-Homestead Book Company, 1974.

Holland Purchase History Society. *History of Genesee County, New York, 1890-1982.* Interlaken, New York: Heart of the Lakes Publishing, 1985.

Huxford, Sharon and Bob. *Huxford's Collectible Advertising: Second Edition.* Paducah, Kentucky: Collector Books, A Division of Schroeder Publishing Company, Inc., 1995.

_____ *Schroeder's Antiques Price Guide: Fourteenth Edition.* Paducah, Kentucky: Collector Books, A Division of Schroeder Publishing Company, Inc., 1996.

Interbrand Group. *World's Greatest Brands: An International Review.* Hong Kong: John Wiley & Sons Inc., 1992.

Jorgensen, Janice. *Encyclopedia of Consumer Brands.* Detroit, Michigan: St. James Press, 1994.

Martin, Rick and Charlotte. *Vintage Illustration: Discovering America's Calendar Artists.* Portland, Oregon: Collectors Press, Inc., 1997.

McGrath, Molly W. *Top Sellers, U. S. A.* New York, New York: William Morrow and Company, Inc., 1983.

Miller, C. L. *Jewel Tea Grocery Products with Values.* Atglen, Pennsylvania: Schiffer Publishing, Ltd., 1996.

Mirabile, Lisa. *International Directory of Company Histories,* Volume II. Chicago, Illinois: St. James Press, 1990.

Morgan, Hal. *Symbols of America.* New York, New York: Viking Penguin Inc., 1986.

Nicholston, Susan B. *The Encyclopedia of Antique Postcards.* Radnor, Pennsylvania: Wallace-Homestead Book Company, 1994.

Olsen, Frank H. *Inventors Who Left Their Brands On America.* New York, New York: Bantam Books, 1991.

Room, Adrian. *NTC's Dictionary of Trade Name Origins.* Chicago, Illinois: NTC Business Books, 1994.

Reed, Walt and Roger. *The Illustrator in America 1880-1980.* New York, New York: Madison Square Press Inc., 1984.

Reno, Dawn E. *Advertising Identification and Price Guide.* New York, New York: Avon Books, 1993.

Rhode Island State Bureau of Information. *The Book of Rhode Island.* Rhode Island Conference of Business Associations, 1930.

Stipanovich, Joseph. *City of Lakes: An Illustrated History of Minneapolis.* Woodland Hills, California: Windsor Publications, Inc., 1982.

Stivers, David. *The Nabisco Brands Collection of Cream of Wheat Advertising Art.* San Diego, California: Collectors' Showcase, Inc., 1986.

Turner, Jean W. *Collectible Aunt Jemima Handbook & Value Guide.* Hong Kong: Schiffer Publishing, Ltd., 1994.

Trager, James. *The Food Chronology: A Food Lover's Compendium of Events and Ancedotes from Prehistory to the Present.* New York, New York: Henry Holt and Company, Inc., 1995.

Watkins, Julian L. *The 100 Greatest Advertisements 1852-1958: Who Wrote Them and What They Did.* Mineola, New York: Dover Publications, Inc., 1959.

Wood, James P. *The Story of Advertising.* New York, New York: The Ronald Press Company, 1958.

Index